RESIN
ALCHEMY

INNOVATIVE TECHNIQUES FOR MIXED-MEDIA AND JEWELRY ARTISTS

SUSAN LENART KAZMER

INTERWEAVE.
interweave.com

editor Marlene Blessing
technical editor Jane Dickerson
designer Karla Baker
photographer Joe Coca
photo stylist Ann Swanson
production Katherine Jackson

Interweave Press LLC
A division of F+W Media, Inc.
201 East Fourth Street
Loveland, CO 80537
interweave.com

Manufactured in China by RR Donnelley Shenzhen

Library of Congress Cataloging-in-Publication Data

Kazmer, Susan Lenart.
Resin alchemy : techniques for mixed-media
and jewelry artists / Susan Lenart Kazmer.
    pages cm
Includes index.
ISBN 978-1-59668-644-1 (pbk)
ISBN 978-1-62033-463-8 (PDF)
1. Jewelry making. 2. Mixed media (Art) 3.
Gums and resins, Synthetic. I. Title.
TT212.K393 2013
745.594'2--dc23

                              2012048060

10 9 8 7 6 5 4 3 2 1

ACKNOWLEDGMENTS

After a time of many changes, I am so very blessed in my life to have all of the right people around me now.

Thank you to Marlene Blessing, who worked side by side with me to finally transform my ten-year body of work exploring the alchemy of resin into a finished book. Through our collaboration, I had the opportunity to witness her brilliance.

Thank you to my wonderful children, who through all of our hard work and changes have come out on the other side happier, healthier, and smarter.

Thank you to Jen Cushman, who has stood by my side in business and in health and who has worked to help build our incredible business. Thank you also to the whole Ice Resin design team, past and present, for continuing to create innovative work and for helping to make Ice Resin an incredible medium.

I hope my readers will be as inspired as I have been by exploring resin. Here's to creativity without limits!

CONTENTS

INTRODUCTION
Endless Possibilities for Designing with Resin

Someone asked me recently how I would describe myself as an artist. I answered that I consider myself first and foremost an explorer. I search for visual clues, found objects, stories, history, and media that allow me to create meaningful art objects. As a mixed-media artist, I'm always looking for materials I can incorporate that will push my work to the next level. At this point in my artistic journey, resin really excites me. When I choose a medium, I can't help but immerse myself in it. With resin, I've mixed it with my metalwork, carved it, cast it, applied it to fabric and paper, colored it with mica to create cold enamel, and more.

Like most people, I was fascinated early on with natural resins, such as turtle shell and amber. Seeing an ancient bug preserved in a piece of amber was amazing and beautiful to me. While my passion for resin was in full force, I attended a popular— and controversial—museum exhibit, Body Works. I was both mesmerized and repulsed as I viewed the exhibit's human bodies, cadavers that had been preserved with a resinous plastic. Here, the body's musculature, bones, ligaments, and more

My award-winning *Key to Freedom* sculpture incorporates ordinary objects such as locks, hardware, and twigs with wire and resin. Photo by Michelle Monet.

were revealed in all their raw nakedness. Many of the once-live bodies were posed in dance and sports positions and body parts were bisected, revealing some of the beneath-the-skin mysteries of the human body. I learned that resin can encapsulate anything and even preserve an object for eternity.

Transform the Ordinary with Resin

In *Resin Alchemy*, I hope to inspire you to explore the many dimensions of resin.

Why alchemy? Because, when combined with other materials, resin is a substance that transforms them by making them more than they were. It's magical. It can strengthen fragile organic matter that would otherwise deteriorate, such as dried leaves. It can turn ordinary paper into a mysterious and translucent material. It can be layered to create dimension: pour some over a piece of fabric nestled in a bezel, let it set; then sprinkle glitter and pour in more resin. Resin can create a beautiful time capsule with words, objects, and other elements suspended within it. Transformation!

This is my *Poker Game* necklace. Cut-up dollar bills, pencil stubs, miniature playing cards—anything goes when you work in mixed media. Photo by Michelle Monet.

Actual resin techniques are easy to master. The art of working with resin, discovering its limits, and achieving beauty requires time and patience. It also requires learning how to "see." Found objects are a central ingredient in my designs. I've used such unlikely finds as broken pencil stubs, cigarette butts, poker cards, a $100 bill, sticks, the bones of birds, sand from a Caribbean beach, seashells, peacock feathers, and eggshells. (See "Talismans, Amulets, Relics, and Prayer Boxes" on page 36 for a more in-depth discussion of how found objects can be incorporated in resin art.) For me, seeing is imagining. *What story can this object tell?* I ask myself. Sometimes, I only know that I need to collect an object and keep it around me until it speaks to me. Once I feel the story emerge, I know that I have achieved the first 5 percent of my work. The remaining 95 percent comes from applying all the skill and craft I have to make it my own. That's another kind of alchemy.

Find Creative Freedom

To see these dynamic and unusual possibilities in ordinary objects, you have to relax into freedom and flow. You knew this freedom when you were a child. You could create wild, make-believe stories using anything you found in your surroundings—for example, sticks, string, stones, feathers, cardboard boxes, buckets, nests. You can recapture this freedom when you combine resin and mixed-media material with found objects. But it's not all about inspiration. To go deeper into a piece, building layers

Jewelry with charms that showcase resin's endless possibilities.

of intricacy to make it memorable, you need to master some jewelry-making skills. Whether you intend your creations to be elegant, whimsical, or fun, they won't be fully realized unless they're put together well structurally and make sense.

When you combine the skill of seeing with good craftsmanship to achieve beautiful depth, you're engaged in the ritual of building art. It's a two-part ritual that I've witnessed many times in my workshops. First, you communicate a feeling, an experience, a story to others. And second, you're making sense of your own life. Sounds big. It is. I tell my students that building pieces is all about solving problems. Another way to approach it is to say that it's about revealing mysteries. It's both.

Observe and Collect

It's so important to keep a collection of your ideas. A sketchbook or journal is truly the best way to do this. My own drawings are very sketchy, not pretty, just simple lines. This allows me to go at the speed of my imagination, so that ideas don't just fly away and evaporate. In addition, I use text, arrows, and symbols to add emphasis to the ideas I record. What's a great surprise is that once you've sketched your ideas, you have automatically sharpened your ability to see found objects that connect to those ideas.

The truth is, you will often reach what you think are dead ends when you are creating. I do that all the time. About 50 percent of people give up at this point, feeling defeated and ready to give up. I encourage you to be part of the other 50 percent.

Yes, you can walk away. And when you get to this point, it is time to walk away . . . temporarily. Get some distance so you can start fresh and imagine new possibilities. You have to move past imperfections, real or imagined, so you can enter the discovery zone. Here's where you'll find surprises, solutions you hadn't expected to find. And here, too, is where you'll start to trust yourself, knowing that you're going to find a way past that dead end.

One of the most satisfying results of pushing forward is that you will discover your artistic voice in the process. You'll also start drawing from the unique content of your life to do your real work, rather than trying to imitate someone else's art (which most of us do in the beginning). In the end, what we are all striving for is to express our own distinct work and voice. When I finished art school, I definitely wanted to get experiences to gain some rich content for my work. Instead of looking at the work of other contemporary artists, I immersed myself in historical research, digging around like an anthropologist to find a timeless array of jewelry-making techniques and designs. I also traveled a lot to places throughout Mexico, Thailand, and South America, where I documented what amulets were all about.

Design with Your Unique Voice
Loaded with history, experiences, art school, and lots of on-the-job training in metalwork, mixed-media, and fiber-art techniques, I was ready to discover my voice, to build work that represented my perspective from growing up in a

A ring bezel filled with resin-coated paper stack.

This old watchcase is an ideal found-object bezel to fill with resin.

particular time and place, and to make my own amulets based on these experiences. Growing up in Chicago, I'd always been inspired by the wear and tear of street life. Even today, when I travel to places such as Paris, I look for the street life and record as many impressions as I can. Resin has helped

Resin preserves a great image as well as touches of glitter and paint.

You can cast noble forms with resin.

Make a book with resin-coated paper and leaves.

RESIN alchemy

Simulate a stone druzy with resin such as the large one in the bezel on the left side of this project.

me preserve these valuable impressions.

Lately, I've been exploring ways to combine resin and paper. I love the translucency of paper covered in resin. I also love how I can use words. Words are such an important element of this technique because they express wishes, intentions, meditations. And on translucent paper, the words just seem to float. I know you'll enjoy your explorations into this realm of resin, to which I've devoted an entire chapter in this book (see Chapter 4, "Freestanding Resin-Coated Forms").

Just as in my classes, I don't offer "recipes" for resin designs within the pages of this book. That is because I want you to collect and incorporate your own meaningful elements—from papers to found-object bezels and more—with a sense of total freedom. What I do offer are step-by-step instructions on particular techniques that will expand your ability to explore resin's design dimensions. After more than a decade of experimenting with this versatile and sophisticated material, I have lots to share—including the fact that I haven't yet run out of fresh discoveries. Resin Alchemy will give you the knowledge, freedom, confidence, and skills to create your most artful, original jewelry using resin.

BASIC
Tools & Materials

The beauty of making resin jewelry is that you can create expressive designs with maximum impact that require only a modest investment in tools and materials—and rudimentary skills. Plus, you can start your journey by simply pouring resin into premade bezels that contain interesting prints, lettering, or other found objects. A small table and a comfy chair near a source of good ventilation is the only "studio" you need to begin.

As you progress, you'll quickly want to master a few metalworking techniques (see Chapter 2, "Basic Metalworking Techniques for Jewelry Design"). Learning these skills will allow you to shape your own bezels and prayer boxes, texture and punch metal wire and sheeting, and create cold connections with eyelets. One tool you'll probably want to invest in if you enjoy metalworking is a flex shaft drill (an electric drill from your hardware store will also work, but will not offer as much control or as many options). The flex shaft is a motor-driven tool to which you can attach many sizes of drill bits, grindstones, cutters, polishing wheels, and more.

As you go through the chapters in *Resin Alchemy*, you can always choose to substitute premade bezels and metal stencils and templates in projects that involve metalworking.

You can't make any mistakes with resin, because mistakes can always be repaired. Overspills can be snipped off with scissors if you fill your bezel a little too full. You can add drying time if your resin isn't completely hard at the end of the initial cure. You can sand the surface once it's dried. This is a forgiving material that allows redos. (See Chapter 7, "Finishes and Fixes.")

RESIN BASICS

Two-part resin, mixing cups, and stir sticks (popsicle sticks or craft sticks)

Sponge and sponge strips

Silicone mold materials

Clear packing tape

Baby wipes and nitrile gloves

Toothpicks

basic tools & materials

ORGANICS

Assemblage of leaves, feathers, sticks, eggshells, etc.

BEZELS

Assorted open-back and closed-back premade bezels

RESIN alchemy

Examples of found-object bezels

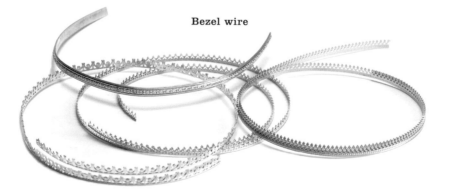

Bezel wire

MATERIALS FOR EMBELLISHMENT AND SURFACE EFFECTS

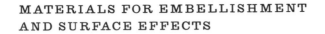

Assorted papers

Permanent-ink stamping pad

Paper sealant

Glitter sheets and tubes of glitter

Embossing powder

Templates, X-Acto knife,
and permanent marker

Gilder's paste

Fine-grit sandpaper

Antiqued rhinestone chain

basic tools & materials

METAL AND
METALWORKING BASICS

Clockwise from upper left: Flat-nose and chain-nose pliers, wire cutters, and long round-nose pliers

Bronze wire in several gauges

Sheet metal

Tubes of eyelets and screws

Heat-resistant tweezers

Clockwise from upper left: Flex shaft and drill bits, Dremel tool, heavy-duty wire cutters, hand files, hole punch, divot punch, metal shears, scissors

Clockwise from upper left: Quenching pan, annealing pan and pumice, and handheld torch

Clockwise from upper left: Metal forming block, dapping punches, ring mandrel, wood dapping block, dapping hammer, and rawhide mallet

Vise

Anvil

Premade bronze templates

basic tools & materials

RESIN COLORING AGENTS

Coloring options and brushes: oil, acrylic, crayon, etc.

Crackle paint

Resin enamel

Resin colored by spices and herbs

Acrylic- *(left)* and oil-colored *(below)* resin

Colored resin with glitter

OTHER HELPFUL ITEMS

Rubber cement

Twine

STIRRED,
NOT SHAKEN:
the art of mixing and pouring resin

You have many choices of resins when you design. All the projects in this book have been created using my Ice Resin product, which I developed with a chemist to be the most versatile and stable resin, as well as the safest. But that doesn't mean you can't choose your own favorite product instead. Here are some of the basics you'll need to understand to help you master the art of mixing and pouring.

Choosing Your Resin

You'll want to select a resin that has excellent clarity so that anything you've embedded within it will show through well (this is especially important when you're showcasing such things as delicate handwriting on yellowed papers, dried flowers with subtle coloration, etc.). Another key quality of the resin you choose: It should not scratch or crack once it is completely cured (three days). And finally, it's great to work with a "self-doming" resin—one that is thick enough when you pour it into your bezel that it will round nicely (if that's the look you want).

Clear resin will highlight the look of embedded materials such as a decorative paper scrap.

Before you choose your resin, check out the Material Safety Data Sheet (MSDS) that is required to be included with every resin. That gives you the lowdown on all the chemicals it contains, together with important product-safety warnings. After all, designing with resin is chemistry first (I like to call it "alchemy"), and you'll want to be sure your resin is the best you can use to create long-lasting art, as well as to ensure your personal health and safety.

Resins that contain polymer or polyurethane are slow-drying products (as long as several days). Gel resins are a quick choice because they dry fast: The downside of this quick-gratification resin is that it is not long-lasting once it has cured. One of the things I value most when I make jewelry and other resin art is that it is durable enough to last a lifetime—at least for my lifetime! If you feel the same way, a gel is probably not for you. There are also some resins that never seem to dry in the center, which makes any finished jewelry vulnerable to damage. Finally, most resins are flammable, another safety consideration!

My jeweler's-quality resin is a two-part liquid product (Part A, resin + Part B, hardener) that you mix together in equal parts. Using equal parts is really important. If you add too much of Part A to the mix, your resin may never harden. And if you add too much of Part B to the mix, your resin will still harden but may yellow over time. No matter what type of resin you use, be sure to follow manufacturer's directions carefully.

Self-doming resin creates a rich look.

Safe Resin Practices

What I love about the resin I've developed is that it is thicker than most other resins, can be domed for interesting shaping, and is completely nontoxic when cured (it has fewer volatile organic compounds [VOCs] than acrylic paint). As with most chemically based substances, you'll want to make sure you're creating your resin alchemy in a well-ventilated area, near windows that can be opened. If that's not possible, use a fan to circulate fumes. A dusty basement corner isn't ideal, because the dust particles will stick to your resin.

When you're working with this sticky substance, you can use silicone-based barrier creams to protect your skin if you have any skin sensitivity. These won't rub off onto other things. Also, it's great to have plenty of baby wipes on hand for any spills or drips that occur—which is bound to happen when you're working with liquids! Finally, it's a good idea to wear safety goggles and a dust mask or respirator (you can find them at your local craft or hardware store) when you're sanding resin or working with any materials that give off airborne particles.

Mixing Magic

Mixing resin is a lot like preparing scrambled eggs. You should mix it briskly with a stir stick for two minutes. Next, I let it sit under a warm light for about five minutes. This process allows most of the bubbles to rise and emerge from the resin. Once you have poured resin into your bezel, be sure to have some straight pins or toothpicks on hand so that when you're through stirring and the resin has settled, you can poke any remaining bubbles in the substance. When you do this, your resin is self-healing and will immediately smooth out, even as the resin mixture begins to harden. And keep in mind that when the resin is later heat-cured, the heat loosens the resin mixture, causing it to thin out—thus eliminating

Mix your two-part resin briskly.

any tiny bubbles that escaped your eye! However, if your design includes having bubbles encased, you can create some by blowing into the resin with a tiny straw and drying the resin at a temperature cooler than 70°F (21°C) to retain them.

About an hour after mixing your resin, depending on the temperature in the room, the liquid will begin to heat up and expand. (You will know because the resin cup will be hot to the touch.) At this point the mixture can no longer be used. When I have excess resin after pouring my bezels, I use it to coat paper: I save the paper to use in future projects.

You just have to be a jewelry "chef" and mix your resin according to product instructions, then clarify the substance by poking out the bubbles. The process is that simple. But, like any process, it takes a few tries to perfect your technique. For your practice runs, use expendable bezels, such as a bottle cap, and don't put anything valuable within them to be encased. Play with simple things such as a tiny scrap of newspaper, a small charm, and maybe some glitter to add pop.

POURING. Once you feel you have the hang of mixing, you're ready to pour. There are practical applications for resin, such as sealing a porous surface like paper. Resin will also strengthen and add body to any organic matter and fragile objects: eggshells and twigs are among those I like to reinforce with resin. Plus, resin is a natural glue. You'll need to be sure to clean any object you plan to encase in resin. Rub organics with alcohol wipes to dry them out and remove any surface dirt. Even metal

pieces that look clean probably still have some machine-oil residue on them. Use both sandpaper and an alcohol wipe to clean these surfaces. Be sure to let them dry thoroughly before incorporating them in your jewelry.

I like to drip resin carefully into my bezel using a wooden stick (a clean stir stick, for example) for greater accuracy and control. I gently tap any objects I've placed in the bezel before the pour. If I have paper in the bezel, I press it to the bottom of the bezel to help release any hidden bubbles. Organic materials, such as spices, sticks, etc., are porous and may contain a lot of bubbles. I check my pieces that are drying after fifteen minutes to make sure that all is well. This is the last check before the dry.

DRYING. The drying process takes about six hours at 70°F (21°C). In this process, the mixture remains sticky, so air bubbles can be released and the mixture can settle. While it dries, you want to keep your resin in a safe place where it will not tip over, spill, or be exposed to floating particles that could land on and become a permanent part of your finished piece. Whether you're drying a thin piece of paper coated with resin or a gallon container filled with resin, the drying time is the same—six hours.

CURING. To the eye, your piece looks finished after drying. While much or all of the finishing work can be performed on resin in its dry state, such as drilling, sanding, layering, and applying surface effects, your finished resin component is not completed until you have cured it. Curing takes about three days. After curing, there will be no more release of VOC (volatile organic compound) gases, and your resin component will be nontoxic.

HEAT DRYING. A resin piece can be placed in a heating unit, such as a dehydrator or a toaster oven at 90° to 135°F (32–57°C) without harming your resin. This accelerates the drying process to one hour. Just let your freshly mixed resin piece sit for half an hour before putting it in the heating unit to allow bubbles to rise to the surface and the mixture to settle.

For the record, I prefer to air-dry my pieces because I work with multiple projects at the same time. This way, my pieces can stay as they lay, undisturbed.

Designing with Resin

Design is where the real fun is; it's where your creativity comes into play. To figure out your design approach, ask yourself some leading questions. For example: What effects do I want—layered, floating, negative and positive space? What kind of bezel will best hold my creation? Do I want subtle or bright coloring or a glasslike, clear effect?

BEZEL. In Chapter 3 ("Creating Simple Bezel Forms for Resin"), I describe how to make several different kinds of bezels. Basically, a bezel is simply a container for the object(s) and materials you want to encase in resin. You can use convenient readymade bezels (which are widely available

For a backless bezel, apply tape to its back side, pour resin, and cure.

A found-object bezel with an embedded photo image.

Resin-coated paper creates a great transparent effect.

I am making resin-coated paper (see page 109), I want to create the effect of gorgeous translucency or transparency that resin does so well. To achieve this, I simply don't put a sealant on the paper.

For the most part, resin will not damage or alter photocopies, pencil drawings, printed text or images, photos, or permanent inks. Water-based inks, such as a ballpoint pen, however, may bleed and lift. In this case, you would need to heat-set your ink with an iron.

ENCASE. Just about everything is fair game for encasing: dried flowers, wet leaves, paper scraps with words on them, small metal springs from old watches, even bugs and grunge. Really! Resin penetrates, stabilizes, and strengthens organic matter. It also preserves porous nonorganic materials.

COLOR. Add colors to your resin for depth and vibrancy: I like to mix in such things as colorful spices, glitter, a dot of oil or acrylic paint (that's all it takes!). Even sand and dirt can inject some cool effects. Oil paint gives color and retains the transparency of the resin, whereas acrylic paint is not as transparent. Oil pastels are fun because they stay nice and bright. In my workshops, I organize groupings of small plastic cups that contain different color ingredients—paints, spices, mica powders, and cold enamel—so students can see the many and varied color effects that different substances create.

at your local bead and craft stores, as well as online). You can also opt for a found-object bezel. And something I've really loved doing lately is creating backless, wireworked bezels. All you have to do is apply tape to the back side of the wire bezel, pour, cure, and remove the tape. A sticky packing tape gives the cleanest back, while duct tape doesn't get sticky, so it tends not to work as well.

EMBED PAPER IMAGES AND TEXT.
Sometimes, you may want to include a photo of a loved one, text from a dictionary, or a love letter found in an attic. Whatever the case may be, you'll need to decide if you want your image and paper to look exactly as it is. Or do you want to create a transparent look? If I want my paper to remain opaque, I simply coat it with Elmer's glue or a water-based paper sealant. This will seal your paper so resin will not seep in. However, most often when

Hollow forms made from resin are among my favorites.

LAYER. You can also layer your resin in stages (pour/dry/pour/dry) to suspend items and effects in the resin at different levels. Techniques such as engraving, cross-hatching, coloring, and embedding objects are ideal to incorporate in layered resin. I use glitter a lot in my pieces for light and shine. This suffuses a piece that has the look of a relic or ruin with contrast or pop. All things in balance!

HOLLOW. What's great about creating hollow forms with resin is that they allow you to give movement to your pieces. I incorporate lots of hollow forms in my own resin jewelry—everything becomes so dynamic with this form. There are many different ways to make a hollow form (see "Resin Hollow Forms," page 98).

Once you feel confident using these simple techniques for mixing and pouring resin, you're on your way to creating innovative designs that capture beauty and movement in a transparent form.

Special Effects:
Decorative Surface Treatments

When I feel I am finished with a resin piece, I always study the piece closely to see if I can add one (or more) final special effect(s). What can I do to make the message of the piece pop? Does it need more texture? More color? More geometry? Some inscribed lines? A patina for the look of antiquity? Sparkle?

Once your resin piece has fully dried, the fun has just begun. You can get even more creative by adding surface treatments to accentuate the look and feel of the piece. You can texture or remove some of the dry resin by sanding, piercing, drilling, carving, engraving, or scratching. Use any one or a combination of these techniques purely for the beauty of the effects they leave behind. For example, there is no function for a decorative drilled hole, other than to look interesting. Go further: You can embellish such a hole by adding a gem or oil pastel for color.

Sand the resin surface for a cloudy, mysterious effect.

ADD SOME SPARKLE. A multifaceted crystal stone loses its sparkle when submerged in resin, because resin's job is to fill in a negative space and smooth it out. Facets placed in wet resin get lost in this process. To retain your stone's facets and their shine, drill a small hole into your dry resin surface. Then, dab a small amount of resin into the negative space and set your stone. Now the stone will sit on the surface permanently and radiate its beauty. Also, the resin glues the stone securely so it will not loosen over time.

ADD A COLORFUL EDGE. For the beauty of it, drill multiple holes around the edges of a resin piece and rub oil pastels into them. This will create a colorful edged border on your piece. Photo transfers, rub-ons, and water-based tattoos can also be rubbed right onto the surface of resin. They become permanent when coated with a thin layer of resin.

ADD OTHER EFFECTS. At this point, you may want to add another layer of color or some text by engraving a word on the dry resin surface. Or perhaps you want to make the piece look more mysterious by sanding the surface to make it cloudy, but translucent.

After incorporating all the surface effects you want and your piece has dried again, it is time to do whatever functional drilling and sanding the piece requires. (See Chapter 7, "No Mistakes: Finishes and Fixes.")

Seven Tips for
Choosing and Combining Objects

Key elements in this mixed-media assemblage are brass tags, scraps of paper printed with words and numbers, and wire coils. Photo by Michelle Monet.

Here are my top tips for building a mixed-media piece that will speak for itself. In choosing and combining your elements, select a focal piece that signifies your theme—a grandmother's photograph, a fragment of a love letter, a foreign stamp, a small seashell. Whatever you choose, your materials should match the intensity of the statement you want your piece to make. What do you want to express? Love for a grandmother? Memories of a spectacular trip? The joy you feel under the summer sun? Anger or sadness over a loss? You want the viewer to look at your piece and immediately grasp what it's about.

This rusted key might open my distorted heart. Photo by Michelle Monet.

One of my favorite pieces is a necklace I made called *The Poker Game*. Growing up in Chicago with my dad, we learned math through real-life experiences, such as poker. This piece expresses everything about how it feels to be sitting in a poker game, wanting to win. The necklace doesn't feature a single piece that isn't related to the subject. Elements include fifty-two playing cards: You can take the piece apart and use these cards to play an actual poker game. There are also betting chips and resin-coated money—in fact, there's a $100 bill in the piece that's cut apart. If you run out of money in a game, you can remove these pieces, tape them together, and you're back in the game! I even included resin-coated cigarette butts. (My dad actually smoked cigars, but I couldn't make cigar butts work.)

1 INCORPORATE A POWERFUL WORD IN THE DESIGN. The viewer's eye should go to one key word that delivers your creative message. Words that are in large type and boldface immediately grab attention. You'll discover favorite words and phrases you prefer to use for their power. The old me liked bad girl. The new me favors words such as transformation, empowering, and beneficial. Your special words will evolve and change over time, charting your personal growth. Oftentimes, I handwrite my words, which can be tricky since they may be hard to read. That suits me just fine, because sometimes I don't want the reader to know what the word is. I want it to be subliminal, beneath the surface. To do this, I might also write a word in a different language or bury it under layers.

2 HAVE A STRONG VISION FOR YOUR DESIGN AND RECORD IT. Your work is very personal and gives you a way to record your vision and experiences. In classes I teach, each of the students brings unique materials for her designs. Before you even mix and pour your resin, lay out all your collage materials and assemble and reassemble them until you've found the arrangement that makes sense to you. Then you can refine the vision by editing, which just means sorting, selecting, and eliminating the inessential. As I work on a piece, I'm in the process of figuring out all the effects I want to achieve. Should it be misty or foggy on the surface to indicate that the subject is a dream? Should it have warm colors or cool colors? When you've made all your choices, write them in a small journal. I have put projects aside when I couldn't complete the vision, then resumed working on them months, even years, later. My journal helps me start where I left off.

3 BUILD A PIECE FROM THE HEART. Building a piece from the heart is what distinguishes art from simple crafting. An artist has to put herself onto the canvas. Every artist knows that when you build a piece from your heart, you are exposing your true self—and that will make you feel vulnerable, maybe even afraid. If you're just following someone else's designs, you can't tap into this: Designing without a script puts you in touch with your unique vision. If thinking about it doesn't work, just go into your work space and start hammering some metal. The strokes you make, the impressions you choose, will allow you to begin creating something in your own voice.

My method for starting the process is to gather information. For example, I took a walk in the spring on the shores of Lake Erie when all kinds of interesting pieces and parts wash up as the lake thaws. No sunny California beach here. This is *my* beach. To represent this jumble, I chose a ribbon, charms, sticks, and shells. These remind me of how things come rolling

Circus themes are among my favorites!

up on the beach. I then connected them by knotting and winding wire and fiber around them, plus I used the same colors I saw and a lot of shells. The piece celebrates a physical memory—nature's passage and how I feel as winter recedes and spring approaches.

4 GATHER RELEVANT PIECES. Pick primary, secondary, and tertiary pieces. Anything can be relevant, as long as it combines naturally with everything else you've chosen to support the idea or feeling you want to express. In my piece titled *A Tribute to the Ba-Conga*, my vision was of a beautiful West African man. In a place where I once worked, I met a lot of African traders. I wanted to create a tribute to these extraordinary men. Some of the most relevant secondary pieces I chose were peacock feathers, measuring tape, bullets, and gears. They were all items that spoke to the unique masculinity, strength, and beauty of these men.

5 CREATE YOUR OWN PERSONAL COLLECTION OF ARTIFACTS. Gather bits that speak to you and keep them on hand until you can hear what the pieces are telling you. When I travel, I pack artifacts I've collected to spread out and view periodically: These make me feel comfortable, reminding me of home or unforgettable places I've been. To select items with meaning, ask yourself: Does it trigger an emotion—happiness, anger, jealousy, fear, excitement? You have to get used to looking inside to develop this "sixth sense" about objects. This was one of the most important lessons I got in art school: Sometimes emotions are uncomfortable, but stay with them. They'll be your creative compass.

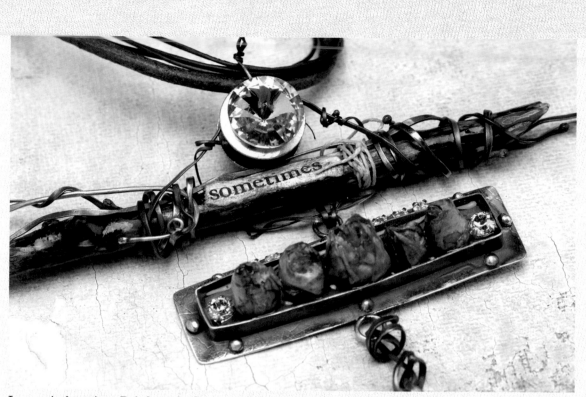

Lesson in layering: Dried rosebuds are mixed with a word, metal, a sparkling crystal, and wood.

6 COMBINE ORGANIC MATERIALS WITH ENGINEERING AND DETAIL. When you're working with organic materials, which can often be fragile, you'll want to make them durable and ready to connect. The piece I've included in this book that incorporates rosebuds is a perfect example (see page 102). First, I needed to coat the rosebuds with resin to preserve them: Resin adds protection and beauty. Next, I thought about how to add my signature to the buds—how should I alter them? Color, graffiti, and gluing glitter or crystals are just a few methods you can use to do this. Last, I had to determine the best way to engineer the connections. I asked myself: Should the rosebuds be glued to a bezel or individual bead caps, drilled, wrapped with wire? Did I want movement in my connections? Form = function.

7 USE DIVERSE SOURCES OF INSPIRATION. If you travel, new or foreign places are excellent sources of inspiration. When I am strolling through the flea markets in Paris, I collect pieces that express the sights and feel of Paris, the city of love. Objects that speak to me include beautiful papers, handwritten love letters, graphics of men and women in love, locks and keys. Romance is always inspiring. On my most recent trip to Paris, I saw a lot of costumes made for the famous Moulin Rouge—silks and laces, bling, etc. In an instant, I saw that this would be an exciting new direction for my designs. But you don't have to travel beyond your own neighborhood or even your own house. A walk down an alley or in a nearby park or maybe by the edge of a lake can yield inspirations from romance to nature to urban garbage. If you keep your eyes and heart open, you'll receive all the messages you need!

Talismans, Amulets, Relics, and Prayer Boxes

An entire neckpiece has been created around a single talisman—worn pencil stubs salvaged from an old-school journalist. Photo by Michelle Monet.

For many years, I've been fascinated by talismanic objects and have studied their history extensively. These human-crafted objects speak to something sacred, beyond the self, and beyond time. And whether they are worn for protection, power, healing, magic, or some other mystical purpose, they are the most ancient of material attempts to reach out for some tangible quality that you may be looking for in your life. My first introduction to ancient relics was a powerful encounter I had when I was a teenager. On a family vacation to San Francisco, we visited the Ripley's Believe-It-or-Not Museum, just for the fun of it. There, among the curiosities, I saw some amazing ancient Tibetan art. I was mesmerized by these artifacts, which were made of the most primitive materials—bones, hair, sticks, shells, rocks. They seemed to be speaking to me.

In the beginning, I was like an anthropologist—exploring, cataloging, researching. The stories and meaning behind these objects were about someone else's rituals—so interesting to study, but definitely outside of me. After I left art school, I traveled to many exotic destinations. In Southeast Asia, I spent time with the hill tribe people of Thailand, for example. There, I saw their skilled artisans create beautiful metal pieces from European coins, using the simplest rustic handmade tools. Some favorite things that I collected during this time were a baby carrier from Thailand, a handmade bell to be hung around a goat's neck, and a collapsible ancient scroll, filled with mystery and documenting cultural traditions from the past.

IT'S ABOUT MEANING. The common denominator embedded in all the talismans, amulets, relics, and prayer boxes I studied was meaning. The materials used, the way a piece was formed, the intention of the maker all combined to express a particular meaning. A while back, my friend and fellow artist Karen Michelle built a piece of artwork for me that incorporated the word *gentle*. When I first received it, I was confused by this choice of word. I kept trying to figure out "Why this word?" Over time, gentle became a kind of mantra or meditation for me. I realized it was a missing element in my life.

FINDING YOUR VOICE. In my first attempts at creating my own talismans, I combined various ethnic looks to create

A resin-coated eggshell half becomes a container for prayers, secrets, or intentions.

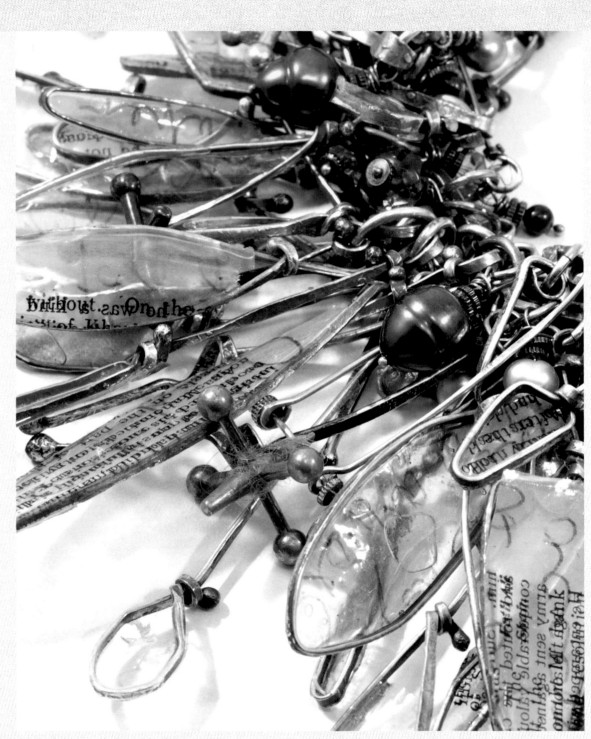

Central talismans in this playful piece are jacks from a child's ball-and-jack game.
Photo by Denise Anderson.

something global. Through the process of making these, I found my own visual "voice." Now, when I make my art pieces, especially prayer boxes, they usually incorporate a word or a thought that is typed, handwritten, or printed text from a book. It is not important to me whether this word or thought is highly visible in the piece or not. It still functions as a talisman. Daily, I record favorite words that I find in the dictionary or a word that just comes to me. These words are very important to my art. When I'm building a prayer box, it's meant to contain a word, which I engrave on the metal. The words I choose are various and changing. Lately, I am using words such as harmony, peace, centered. Like a blind person with a sixth sense, people gravitate to certain pieces. They can't see the word, but they feel it.

COLLECTING AND DISPLAYING. These days, like those ancient artists before me, I surround myself with meaningful objects that carry messages. In fact, sometimes when I'm teaching and moving about in my life, it is important for me to wear my own talismans. I used to wear one of my most powerful talismans made of pencil stubs, a necklace called *Energy Talisman*. Wearing these talismans and prayer boxes is a completion of the piece. In other words, each one does its true work when it is worn, held, or displayed.

FINDING YOUR OWN SPECIAL TALIS-MANS. First, explore your garage, clothing drawers, junk drawers, studio space, etc., to get a good idea of the pieces that you have been drawn to collect and have saved over the years. You may find that they still have a strong significance for you. These pieces may remind you of a happy time in your life, a lucky experience, or perhaps even a love relationship. They all symbolize something that once made you feel good. Looking more closely at these pieces, you may notice that a particular shape recurs, such as a circle. All shapes represent a particular quality.

DISCOVERING YOUR SHAPE. Once, in the 1990s, when I was living on the north side of Chicago, I was building my company, a wholesale higher-end commercial jewelry business. I was focused on the business and moving ahead at a fast pace, and I noticed that the only shape I could produce was a triangle with such sharp points that I was afraid they would hurt my customers. I realized that this quality in the triangle signified the place where I worked. There was artistic balance and focus to the designs, but their sharp points were arrows that signified the energy of urban life.

Here are some qualities represented by the most common but powerful shapes. Everyone is drawn individually to her own shape:

Circle. In most cultures, it represents the endless cycle of life, coming full circle, continuous ideas and flow.

Square and rectangle. Very solid and sturdy forms, these embody strength and grounding.

Triangle. Pointed downward in an arrow, the triangle is a very powerful symbol of strength and power.

Spiral. This dynamic form speaks to movement, moving, and shaking.

Bezel with Interior Crackling

MATERIALS & TOOLS

Handcrafted, purchased, or found-object bezel

Paper image(s) to fit bezel interior

Paper sealant

Brown acrylic paint

Two-part resin, mixing cups, and stir sticks

Paintbrush

Toothpicks

Sponge-strip resin applicator (optional)

X-Acto knife or small scissors

Q-Tip or cotton ball

Paper towel or cloth

Alcohol wipes

Baby wipes

Nitrile gloves

Large white plastic trash bag

I love ancient relics and use various methods to replicate their qualities in my resin pieces. A piece that I relish in my personal treasures is an old broken glass locket with a photo behind it. Through time, the wear of age and dirt have rubbed into the cracks of the glass. To me, this is an exciting piece to replicate. To mimic this effect, I have come up with a series of cross-hatching techniques that can be done in layers or used in a single layer of resin. This technique can also be used to give you the look of stone inclusions (those cool lines that look like fuzzy lightning encased in transparent stone). The trick with this is to score dried resin, rub it with paint, and cover it with more resin. When you're done, it looks natural and aged!

1. Place the plastic trash bag on your work surface. If you're using a handcrafted or purchased bezel, clean it with alcohol wipes and let it dry. Brush your paper image with sealant and place it in the bottom of your bezel. When it has dried, mix and pour the resin on top of your image, filling the bezel about halfway. Using a stir stick, press the paper to the bottom of the bezel to help release any hidden bubbles. (If your bezel is small, using a sponge-strip applicator will allow you to drizzle the resin into it.) Use a toothpick to pop any bubbles.

2. After the resin dries (6 hours), crosshatch and scratch lines deep into the surface of your resin with either small scissors or an X-Acto knife (I often use both). Make sure you scratch both long and short lines to make it look like natural stone inclusions **(Fig. 1)**.

3. Dab a bit of acrylic paint on the surface and rub it into the crosshatch marks and scratches **(Fig. 2)**. The paint will fill these cracks. Be sure to rub the color into the edges as well to add dimension. (I just rub it in with my fingers, but you can use a Q-Tip, a cotton ball, or a paper towel.)

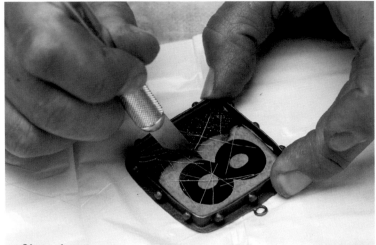

fig. 1

fig. 2

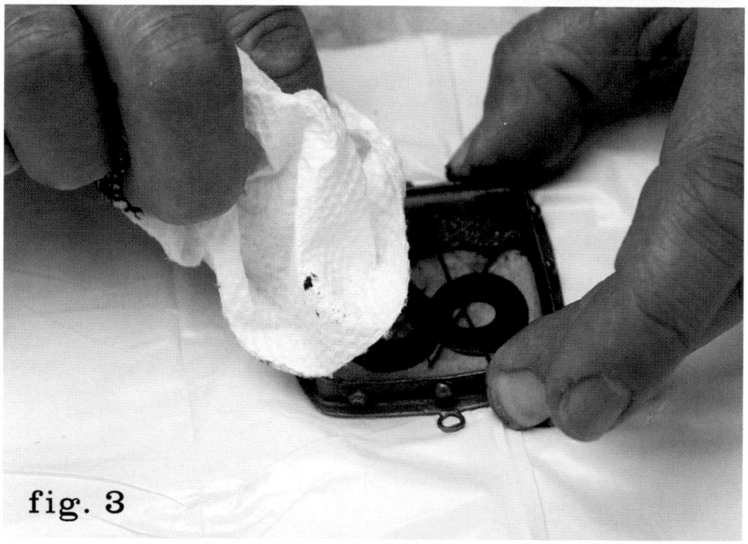

fig. 3

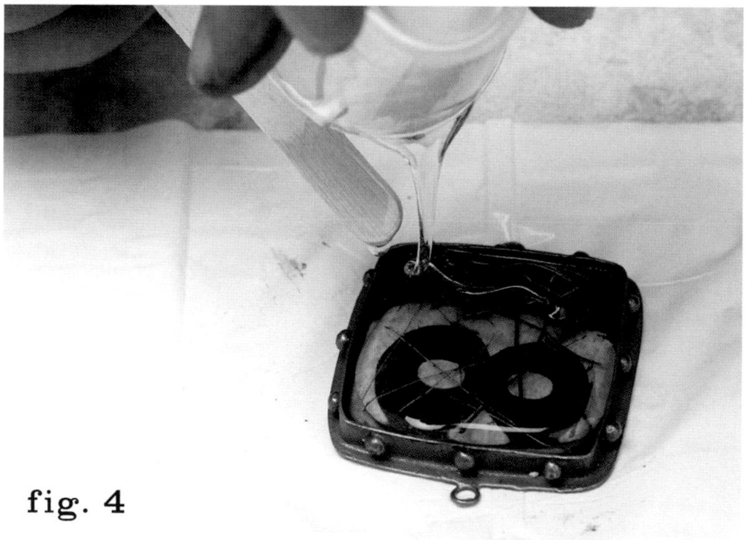

fig. 4

4 If you made any scratches that you decide you don't want, just avoid rubbing them with paint. When you do your second resin pour, these scorings will fill with resin and will not show anymore.

5 Buff and clean the surface with a cloth or paper towel (Fig. 3).

6 After the paint dries, pour in more resin to fill the rest of the bezel to the top (Fig. 4).

NOTE

If you are using an open-back bezel, tape the back with clear packing tape and fill the bottom with a thin coat of resin. (It's important to have clean hands when you do this because any kind of dirt or oily substance will stick to the tape; this will transfer to the resin and will become part of your piece. Even your fingerprints can leave an impression in the resin.) Sink your sealed image into the bezel, pressing out air pockets with a stir stick or something else that's small and blunt.

Bezel with Engraving

MATERIALS & TOOLS

- Open-back oval bezel
- Clear packing tape
- Glitter
- Paper to fit bezel interior
- Paper sealant and paintbrush
- Two-part resin, mixing cups, and stir sticks
- Toothpicks
- Oil pastels or oil paint
- Black permanent marker
- Small metal stencil
- Small pointed tool
- Engraver
- Engraver attachments (optional)
- Paper towel
- Low-grit sandpaper (optional)
- Scissors
- Alcohol wipes
- Baby wipes
- Nitrile gloves
- Large white plastic trash bag

This is an easy technique for carving away negative space, inserting text, or creating a hollow space for an inclusion. Engraving will provide dimension to the layers in your resin pieces, giving them a sophisticated look. I use an inexpensive engraver from the hardware store. Its cutting tip does not move centripetally, so your lines can be intentional and straight (most Dremel tips move centripetally, and I find them difficult to control).

1 Place the plastic trash bag on your work surface. If you are using a nonorganic bezel, clean it with alcohol wipes and let it dry. Place the bezel, wrong side down, onto the sticky surface of a piece of clear packing tape (**Fig. 1**). (It's important to have clean hands when you do this because any kind of dirt or oily substance will stick to the tape; this will transfer to the resin and will become part of your piece. Even your fingerprints can leave an impression in the resin.) Make sure the tape is smooth—any wrinkles or folds will appear in the back of your finished piece.

2 Evenly sprinkle a thin layer of glitter inside the oval to cover; lightly shake the excess glitter onto your work surface (**Fig. 2**).

3 Place the paper in the bottom of the bezel, press with a small pointed tool to fit, and brush the paper with sealant (**Fig. 3**). Let the sealant dry. Next, fill your bezel halfway with resin; use a toothpick to pop any bubbles. Let the resin dry for 6 hours.

fig. 1

fig. 2

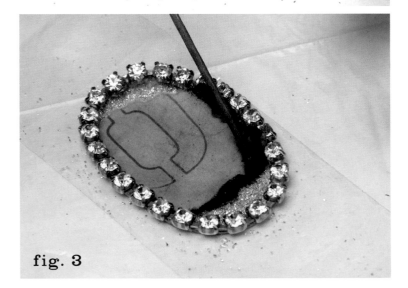

fig. 3

RESIN alchemy

fig. 4

fig. 5

4 Use a black permanent marker to write a word, image, or any text right onto the surface and engrave right over your marker **(Fig. 4)**. (I used a small metal stencil and engraved the number 3 into my resin surface.) Your engraver should have no centripetal (center-seeking) force, allowing you to create nice straight lines. You may also use attachments for your engraving tool.

5 When you have finished engraving, blend oil pastels or paint into the negative space you've created. Rub it in with a paper towel so the paint will remain lodged in the engraved areas **(Fig. 5)**. (Sometimes I repeat this process of adding color a couple times, drying between each addition.)

6 Fill the remaining space in your bezel to the top with resin **(Fig. 6)**; dry (6 hours).

As a finishing touch (optional), you can sand the resin surface lightly with low-grit sandpaper: You'll create a nice clouded translucency.

fig. 6

bezel with engraving

2

MAKE MINE METAL!
basic metalworking techniques for resin jewelry design

Metal is a structurally strong element that goes hand in hand with resin. Because I began my art career as a metalworker, my prejudice is that resin is made more important and substantial with the addition of metal. Whenever possible, I back or encase all my resin jewelry pieces with metal.

Once you begin to get into mixed media in your jewelry making—such as paper, organic materials, and resin—cold joins soon become a big part of your life. Riveting is the most common of all cold-join attachments, but there are other interesting and detailed techniques that you can discover on your own. (See *Making Connections*, my book listed in Resources, page 158.)

You can easily manipulate and drill resin for attachment. If you plan to use a wire attachment through your drilled hole to hang your piece, you must protect your resin with a metal eyelet or tube rivet. Wire would eventually rub away your resin because, as metal, it is far stronger than resin. To create durable and lasting attachments in your jewelry work, always think "metal to metal," with your resin material sandwiched in between.

The techniques that follow demonstrate some ideas to create secure and permanent attachments for your jewelry components. When you add metal to your resin designs, they will definitely last your lifetime. After you've learned the basic metalworking techniques in this chapter, you will be able to build anything pictured in this book. More than that, you'll be able to realize many more of the unique designs you imagine creating.

An example of a metal-to-metal cold connection with resin sandwiched in between.

TECHNIQUE:
Eyelets

MATERIALS & TOOLS

Layers of resin-coated paper and sheet metal

Handheld or electric drill, with 1/16" (2 mm) or 1/8" (3 mm) drill bit

Anvil or bench block

Chasing hammer

Center punch

Eyelet, 1/16" (2 mm) or 1/8" (3 mm) to match drill bit

Metal eyelets are very similar to tube rivets, but much easier to set in a piece of jewelry. I used to set all my jewelry with tube rivets until, one day, I taught a workshop for a paper journaling group and was introduced to a simpler form. An eyelet tube rivet holds pieces together while creating a hole through which wire or other threadlike material can be looped to suspend a component. Eyelets come in standard sizes that correspond with drill- bit sizes, 1/16" (2 mm) or 1/8" (3 mm). There are three tube-length options for eyelets: short, medium, and long. Use the tube length that matches the thickness of your resin piece best, allowing for a small extra margin.

1   You can use either a handheld or an electric drill to make a hole through layers of resin-coated paper and metal: A hole punch will not work effectively. Place your drill bit perpendicular to the surface of the paper and metal layers at the exact point where you want to place the eyelet (Fig. 1). At a low speed, drill gently through the layers of resin and metal to create a hole. Slip the smaller end of the eyelet (the one without a lip) through the hole you've just drilled so that the eyelet lip is on the top of the layers.

fig. 1

2   Lay your piece on an anvil with the nonlipped end of the eyelet facing up and protruding through the layers a couple of millimeters. Place a center punch inside the eyelet end and, with the flat end of your hammer, tap the eyelet tube end gently a couple times to flare it. Finish by tapping the tube end lightly with the ball end of your hammer to ensure an even flare (Fig. 2). These eyelets will protect your resin piece from abrasion whenever the wire that you thread through it moves.

fig. 2

TECHNIQUE:
Nut-and-Screw Rivets

MATERIALS & TOOLS

Sheet metal

Steel nut-and-screw set

Handheld or electric drill with drill bit that matches screw diameter

Metal shears

Ball-peen hammer

Anvil or bench block

Metal file

The nut-and-screw rivet is the easiest of all. Because rivets need contact surfaces to be metal to metal, the nut is the essential piece that solves that problem. The other great feature of this style of rivet is that it has an industrial look and can be purely decorative. Keep in mind that because you're using steel hardware for your rivet, you should use tools from the hardware store, not jewelry-makers' tools.

1. When drilling your hole, drill straight down and perpendicular to your metal—not at an angle.

2. If you plan to rivet multiple metal components together, they must be drilled together so that the holes are aligned precisely.

3. Insert your screw through the hole you've drilled, going from front to back of the sheet metal; screw the nut onto the other end at the back of the piece. (If you want the nailhead to be a prominent feature of the design, you can reverse the order and screw from back to front of the piece.)

4. Cut the excess screw shaft off, leaving just enough to form a nailhead. File the cut end so the tip is level; this will give you a nice, clean rivet. *Note:* If you cut the screw too high, the shaft will not bend when you hammer to create the nailhead, and if it is too low, there won't be enough shaft to form a nailhead. Strike with the flat end of your hammer until the nailhead is completely flat.

5. With the round end of the hammer, strike the rivet very gently and repeatedly in an outward pulling motion; the pulling motion will spread the rivet and make the connection more secure.

Work-Hardening, Annealing, and Drawing a Bead

I like my wire to be wild—meaning, I usually add some irregularities to give it interesting character. To do this, I flatten and texture it with a hammer. I also like to wrap the textured wire freely as if it were fiber, which requires that I anneal it. Another technique that adds flavor—and is practical—is to use the torch to heat the end of the wire until it draws up into a bead. You can make the beads evenly round (once you get the technique down) or give them a funkier look to match your free spirit.

WORK-HARDENING
When wire or sheet metal is hammered, it loses some flexibility and becomes "work-hardened." It must be annealed to bring back that flexibility.

ANNEALING To return work-hardened metal to its former flexible state, evenly fire (anneal) it until it turns red all over. Then cool the metal by grasping it with tweezers and quenching it in a bowl of water.

DRAWING A BEAD
When the tip of the wire gets very hot, the molten metal draws up into a bead. Remove your torch as soon as that happens so the bead remains attached to the wire. Then quench it in a bowl of water.

TECHNIQUE:

Dapped Sheet-Metal
Bezel

Denise Anderson

MATERIALS & TOOLS

Die-cut metal circle (available from any jewelry-supply company)* 1"–3" (2.5–7.5 cm) circumference

Two-part resin, mixing cups, and stir sticks

Toothpicks

Sponge-strip resin applicator

1/16" (2 mm) eyelet

Handheld torch and fuel

Annealing pan and pumice

Fireproof work surface

Heat-resistant tweezers

Quenching pan

Dapping block with dapping punches (wood or metal)

Ball-peen hammer (optional)

Rawhide mallet (optional)

Vise (optional)

Sandpaper

Needle file

Handheld or electric drill, with 1/16" (2 mm) drill bit

Center punch

Sharpie permanent marker

Paper towels

Large white plastic trash bag

Alcohol wipes

Baby wipes

Nitrile gloves

*If you're a skilled jeweler, you can cut your own circular form out of sheet metal.

A dapped bezel will give you a great canvas for using resin with small bits that tell a story or express a feeling. If you want a bold piece, consider using a larger die-cut metal circle. Also, if you have a variety of tiny elements to encase in the resin, you'll want to dap with progressively smaller punches until you have the bezel depth you require.

1   Use sandpaper or a file to clean your metal circle. (All machine-tooled dies will have a residue of machine oil on them, which can impair adhesion. This process removes that.)

2   Place your metal circle on the annealing pan surface. Using a circular motion with your torch, heat the metal evenly until it turns a dull red (Fig. 1). (Do not heat beyond this point.) Quench and dry. Your circle is now flexible and ready to be dapped.

3   Place your metal circle onto your dapping block, centering it over the hollow you've chosen, and tap it gently but firmly once or twice with a dapping punch or the ball end of a ball-peen hammer (Fig. 2). If you want your bezel to be deeper with higher sides, continue dapping in a hollow that is one size smaller than the previous hollow.

4   When your metal circle has been dapped into the depth and cup shape you prefer, you're ready to fill it with your story elements. Clean the metal circle with alcohol wipes and let it dry (Fig. 3). Place the plastic trash bag on your work surface. Mix and pour the resin into the bezel, doming the resin if you choose (see page 24).

fig. 1

fig. 2

fig. 3

RESIN alchemy

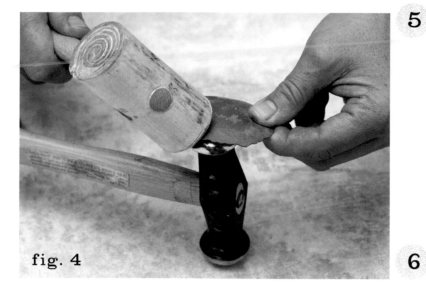

fig. 4

NOTE

You can substitute a ball-peen hammer for the dapping block. Simply place it in a vise to keep it stable and use a rawhide mallet to hammer the metal circle into a cupped shape **(Fig. 4)**.

5 When your piece is dry after 6 hours, mark the spot where you want to create a connection and drill a hole with a 1/16" (2 mm) drill bit. Hold your resin piece firmly with pliers without teeth. Drill speed should be slow and steady to get the best results. Hold the drill straight up and down, perpendicular to the piece, to drill straight through the resin and metal.

6 Insert a 1/16" (2 mm) eyelet into the hole you've drilled and set the back of the eyelet using the center punch (see eyelet instructions, page 51). The eyelet will protect the resin from being worn down over time. Your bezel is ready to attach with wire or string.

dapped sheet-metal bezel

Resin:
A Wonder Glue for Connections

Resin is one of the best bonding glues for metal and other materials. It is possible to construct a whole piece and hold it together permanently using a cold-join attachment created by resin. You may want to wear gloves while applying it. If you do get a bit of resin on your skin, simply remove it with an alcohol wipe.

The resin I work with is an epoxy resin. This is absolutely the best type of glue for holding two pieces together permanently, regardless of what the materials are. Here are the basic reasons you'll want to know about using resin for this practical purpose:

1 Resin is stronger than regular jeweler's glue for adhering surfaces of like or different materials. Also, Ice Resin isn't toxic.

2 Resin can be used to connect metal to metal. (If resin with this strength had existed twenty years ago, many of today's professional jewelry makers would not have a prejudice against using glue.)

3 Although not always recommended, you can substitute resin gluing for soldering metal. All you need to do is apply a thin layer of resin to a clean, sanded surface. If you plan to oxidize the metal, you can do that after the resin dries.

4 To apply resin, use a toothpick. You can also use a toothpick to remove any excess resin before it dries. Plus, just roll some sandpaper around the tip of

The metal wire in this ring is securely glued to the metal disc with resin.

the toothpick to create a handy sanding tool that will work well in hard-to-reach spaces.

5 When you're gluing metal with resin, place your piece in a vise to dry.

6 If there are any resin gaps, just add fresh resin to fill them.

Wire + Resin =
Favorite Combinations

The award-winning, freeform wire styles for which I am known were inspired years ago. To make a living, I was doing jewelry repair at a Chicago-based jewelry company. In my free time, I studied ethnographic jewelry. (Many artists interested in jewelry during the early 1990s were doing similar research.) I studied the beads, metals, and religious properties of ancient jewelry at the Field Museum in Chicago. I wanted to see how these pieces were attached and bound with the simple rustic materials available in those times. I also noted how well these pieces had held up over the ages. Then I adapted these same kinds of attachment techniques—winding, wrapping, and knotting—into my own wireworking.

Letters to My Lover is one of my favorite hollow-form resin rings. Photo by Denise Anderson.

Beginning with a round wire, I hammered it flat, then annealed it to make it dead-soft. This wire was then as malleable as butter. I could manipulate my wire in the same way as I would thread or fiber. My discovery launched a new wire technique and style for me that I like to call "metal fiber" (which refers to the transformed wire) or bird's-nest wire (which refers to the finished look).

I didn't originally think of myself as a wire person. That was before I realized that wire is the backbone for connecting my jewelry and art-object components. Now wire is one of my favorite media. And, like any medium I work with, I push the limits to discover as many design possibilities as I can. For the look of antiquity and timelessness that I desire, bronze wire is my favorite choice (plus it's far less expensive to work with than silver). I also use steel wire to create a silver look—again saving money.

Recently, I began enjoying the raw look of hand-hammered wire paired with the beautiful shiny look of fresh clear resin. The contrasting effects of these combined materials create the perfect balance when building a "relic."

Here are some of my top ways to express my wire side when I'm designing with resin:

CREATE A HOLLOW WIRE FORM FOR RESIN. A birdcagelike hollow form made of shaped and twisted wire is a beautiful thing! In my *Letters to My Lover* ring on page 59, I covered my wire form with resined paper after placing my message inside. This is just another form of a letter in a bottle: You create it in hopes that the message will be released into the world

Sides of this wire bezel were built up with packing tape before pouring resin.

and reach its destination! (See Chapter 4, "Freestanding Resin-Coated Forms," for detailed information on hollow forms.)

MAKE A WIRE BEZEL. To make a wire bezel, I work with a range of gauges, from 8 to 18. I hammer the wire and, if it's a thin 18-gauge wire, I do end up with a lot of negative space after I've wrapped the wire into layers. To ensure that liquid resin does not leak out through the wire and create an unintended bezel wall, I wrap clear packing tape around the outside of the wire bezel and coat the inside of the wire with resin. Once it's dry, I just remove the tape and a transparent wall now fills those holes neatly. I can also build extra shanks or interior walls to create a cloisonné effect.

ADD A WIRE CONNECTION TO A RESIN COMPONENT. When you connect resin components with wrapped wire, a wire stem, or a wire rivet, you protect your more delicate pieces. That's because the wire creates sturdy and lasting connections that let your pieces move. When your pieces are movable, the wire absorbs the stress. Wire connections are especially important for my resin journals. Freeform resin pieces are special favorites of mine, and I often drill directly though the resin pieces and add a wire stem to make a strong connection.

MAKE A "METAL FIBER" FROM WIRE. I enjoy infusing my pieces with an organic look—as if they were created by nature. Oftentimes, I hammer wire flat, heat it to make the wire ball up at one end, then anneal it so that the wire is malleable, like a fiber. I then wrap this wire into a "bird's nest." It's also fun to hammer wire flat into a metal "ribbon" that I can use as a wire tie or wrap.

MAKE THIN SHEET METAL FROM WIRE. You can hammer 8-gauge wire into sheet metal about ¼" (6 mm) thick. The hammering textures the sheet metal to give it that cool worn look I favor in my designs. These can be shaped into bracelets or necklaces or used as the spine structure for a journal.

Best of all, mixing wire with resin to give pieces support, texture, and a material counterpoint to resin gives me lots of options for design improvisation! Once you've tried some of these options, you'll see how "connected" wire is to resin.

Wire that's been hammered flat can be wrapped like ribbon.

Scrolled
Prayer Box

MATERIALS & TOOLS

1" x 2" (2.5 x 5 cm) die-cut 24-gauge sheet metal oval

Two lengths of 20- or 22-gauge wire, about 4"–5" (10–12.5 cm) each

Small brass nut

Resin-coated paper

Brown permanent-ink stamp pad

Crayon or oil pastel stick

Fine-tipped Sharpie pen

String or fiber

Scissors

Sandpaper

Needle file

Dapping punch

Ball-peen hammer

Forming block (optional)

Bench block or anvil

Round-nose pliers

Handheld torch and fuel

Annealing pan and pumice

Fireproof work surface

Heat-resistant tweezers

Quenching pan

Handheld or electric drill, with 1/16" (2 mm) drill bit, or metal hole punch

Wooden or metal dowel

When I teach this project, I give my students two primary tasks. One is to decide the idea to place within the prayer box. This is embodied in a word that describes some quality that you want to bring into your life. The second major task in this project is to use simple metalworking techniques—hammering— to form the metal scroll that will encase your treasured idea.

1. Use sandpaper or a metal file to clean your metal oval. (All machine-tooled dies will have a residue of machine oil on them; this process removes that.)

2. I use dapping punches, but you can use any wooden or metal dowel to form your metal shape. Curve the metal oval lengthwise around your wood or metal dowel with your hands. Next, with the flat end of the hammer, curl the metal tighter on the forming block, leaving a nice opening to view the paper you'll be inserting next **(Fig. 1)**. (If you don't have a forming block, a bench block or anvil will work fine.)

3. Tear a piece of resin-coated paper about the size of your oval metal piece **(Fig. 2)**. I always write a message or word in indelible ink on the inside of my paper so that I'm wrapping an intention, mantra, or idea within this metal scroll.

fig. 1

fig. 2

RESIN alchemy

fig. 3

4 Rub the edges of the resin-coated paper onto the surface of a brown permanent-ink stamp pad to create an aged look **(Fig. 3)**. I like to mix coloring media, so the next step is to use a crayon or oil pastel stick to add a second color (usually brighter) over the browned edges. A final surface treatment is to write a word onto the paper with a fine-tipped Sharpie pen. (*Truth* was my chosen word for this example.)

5 Roll the paper as tightly as possible to create a paper scroll that will fit neatly inside the metal scroll. Once you have tested the fit of your scroll, tie a string or fiber around your scroll and cut to trim the ends **(Fig. 4)**. Rub some color onto your scroll, then gently slide it into the metal scroll's opening, inserting from the top **(Fig. 5)**.

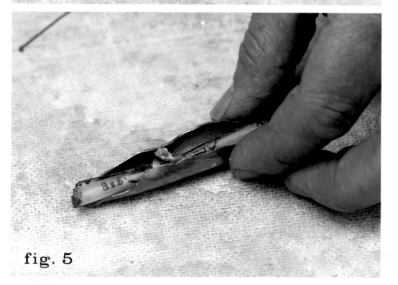

fig. 4

fig. 5

6 Ball one piece of wire at both ends (see page 54). Wrap the wire around the upper third of the scroll and twist loosely to close **(Fig. 6)**.

7 Drill (or hole-punch) a hole in the center of the scroll, straight through the metal and paper **(Fig. 7)**. Then, drill two more holes equidistant from the center hole. (The scrolled prayer box can be attached at both ends to other components and be used as a link, or it can dangle from chain or fiber as a focal piece.)

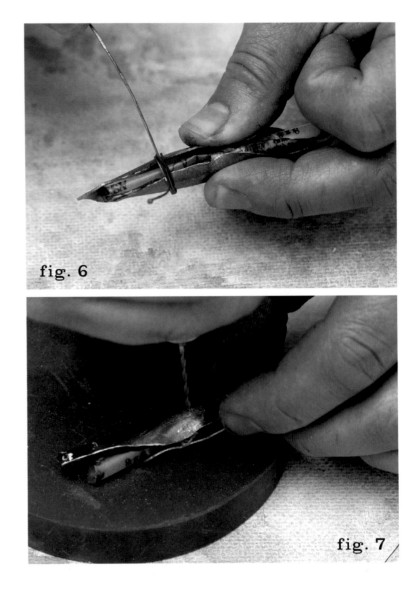

fig. 6

fig. 7

RESIN alchemy

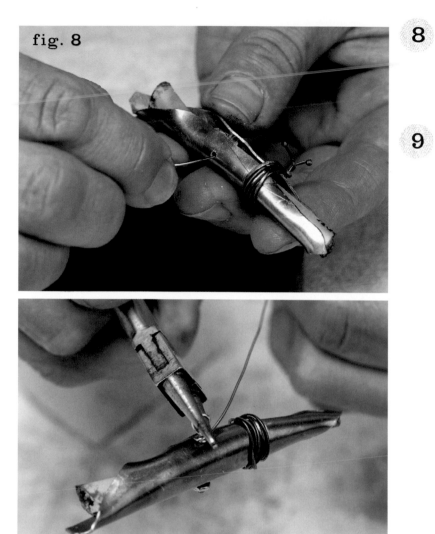

fig. 8

fig. 9

8 Ball one end of the remaining piece of wire. Hold a small nut over the center hole and thread the nonballed end of the wire through it **(Fig. 8)**.

9 Create a wrapped loop with the free end of the wire, using the round-nose pliers **(Fig. 9)**.

CONTAIN YOUR ENTHUSIASMS:
creating simple bezel forms for resin

Bezels are the very foundation into which liquid resin can be poured. Types of bezels vary greatly in terms of material and shapes. Normally, they are constructed of metal, but I have also used zippers, eggshells, wire, and seashells—anything that has a cup shape or depression.

Bezels do not even need to have a back because clear packing tape can be placed over the back opening and serve as a false back. Simply pour in the resin and later remove the tape when your resin piece is dry. These open-back bezels are my specialty and a favorite of mine because their transparency allows the greatest amount of light to pass through, creating a beautiful and bright effect.

When you first begin working with resin, there are lots of manufactured bezels that will be just fine for your early designs. This way you can focus on perfecting your mixing, pouring, and organizing. These commercial bezels may be made of fine metals, such as sterling silver, or more affordable base metal or mixed-metal bezels. Midrange metals include white bronze, bronze, brass, and copper.

Bezels are simply containers or frames that should be chosen carefully to encase your artifacts and collectibles. As you go deeper into the art of resin and become more skilled, you will find that you want to make your own unique bezels from

Found objects as bezels offer one-of-a-kind forms.

metal and organic materials. (Those of you who are already familiar with metalworking will probably make your own bezels at an early stage or already have some that you can begin using with resin.)

The Joy of Found-Object Bezels

Bezels made from found objects produce some of the most surprising, one-of-a-kind forms and are fun to create. First, you'll have to develop a good eye for selecting found objects with potential to become a bezel. And second, you'll have to learn techniques to reinforce some of the more delicate materials—especially organic ones that are porous. Acorns, hollow sticks, eggshells, and any type of wood material are all examples of organic found objects you can transform into bezels. You can even carve pages of a book into a bezel shape. As long as these porous materials are sealed well, they will support and hold resin: You simply coat the inside with Elmer's glue or paper sealant. When it's dry, you can pour in your resin: The water-based sealant will hold all your resin with no leakage. To keep the authentic matte look of the surface of an organic material, such as a twig or an acorn, you can lightly sand the dried resin coating. And if a found object doesn't have four walls, I will show you how to build walls using tape (see page 85).

There are interesting and beautiful alternatives to making a metal bezel besides soldering one together. You can make simple and successful metal bezels of your own by cutting metal tubing from the hardware store, hand-hammering wire and shaping it into a form with walled sides, or using bezel wire from a jewelry-supply source. These are all easy metalworking options that require only a few tools and very simple techniques. The projects I've included in this chapter, in combination with the essential cold joins from Chapter 2, will fully introduce you to the art of bezels.

Backless Wire Bezels

In much of my most recent work, I have enjoyed building backless wire bezels. If you roll your wire through a rolling mill or purchase flat wire, your look will be very clean. However, I like to evoke the sense of a relic, so I hammer out my wire to produce irregularities. The hammering varies the texture and width of the wire, making it look like something that has been weathered through time. I use anything from

Wire bezels such as this heart create a glasslike interior to showcase embedded objects.

16-gauge wire in multiple layers all the way up to a very heavy 8-gauge wire, which yields a thick, tall wire bezel. To complement this rustic look, a precision image sealed in resin serves as a counterpoint and balances the design: I want to make sure my work inside the bezel is clean and bright. Often I use rhinestones, glitter, or even diamonds to do so.

Transparency is another effect that adds light, mystery, and balance to the heavy look of metal jewelry components. I like to design with negative spaces that I cut into my sheet-metal bezel forms with a jewelry saw. (You can also use metal sheet shapes with precut negative spaces.) After the spaces have been cut into the metal, I place tape on the back of the piece, which gives the resin support until it dries. These spaces allow me to make resin "windows" that can showcase a captured word or color or image. Or the windows can simply be clear, allowing light to show through.

In the bezel projects that follow, you'll learn how basic bezel-making techniques will give you many design options for your resin pieces. And whether you choose to work with bronze, copper, nickel, or silver sheet metal, you'll be able to create beautiful jewelry components that will tell your story and reflect your own personal aesthetic.

Resin poured into negative spaces adds balance to metal components.

Tips on Building Mixed-Media Resin Collages

Mixed-media collage involves freely combining any and all kinds of materials that you want to use in building a piece. Materials can be as varied as straw, hair, glass, metal charms or objects, photos, transparencies or transfers, rub-ons, ribbons, shells—anything. In my workshops, I usually guide my students to work on a single theme for each collage piece. To do this, start with one primary object and build your piece with this in mind. For instance, when I built a piece called *Beach Walk*, I carefully chose objects and images that reminded me of a particular beach experience—sticks, twigs, shells, beach-washed twine, rocks, and so on.

My *Beach Walk* necklace reminds me of a special experience by the shore. Photo by Michelle Monet.

Glitter, rhinestones, and color add layering and interest to this heart bezel.

Say you choose an image or picture of a loved one as your inspiration and build your piece from there. If it is an image of your grandmother, maybe you will incorporate a piece from a dress she wore, a label from her favorite perfume, a word in text that reminds you of her. These objects can all be placed in resin to create a meaningful finished piece. Before you pour your resin, make sure that the piece has balance, good use of color, and that the arrangement communicates the message you intend.

When you are building a mixed-media collage, here are important tips to expand your options and ensure your success:

Color
You can color your resin, as well as add colors to the materials you place in your collage.

OIL PAINT. Oils are the most transparent of any pigment in resin, while still providing color. Lift out a tiny bit of oil paint on a toothpick and mix it into your resin. Suspend a mixing swirl of color in resin or blend it in perfectly.

INKS. Inks are transparent, too, but you will not likely achieve the vibrancy of oil paint with them.

ACRYLIC PAINT. Acrylic offers nice, dense color that blends evenly, depending on how much you add to your mixture. Experiment with different amounts to see what you like best.

MICA POWDER. Mica is a surprisingly light metal material. The best thing about mica is that you get a great metallic look without adding heaviness, no matter how much you mix in your work. It catches light well to add beauty and shimmer. Mica can be purchased in forms from fine, glitterlike flakes to larger flakes. It can be used in small amounts or in larger amounts to create the look of beautiful cast-metal objects. One technique I use

Use a toothpick to pop unwanted bubbles.

is to highlight the edges of rice grains, eggshell bits, or random material with small particles of mica powder. (All you need is a tiny amount because the colorations of mica are more concentrated than in paint.) I just place the material in a small cup and add the powder, which sticks to the edges of the grains and bits. When you add the rice to a bezel and pour clear resin over it, you'll love the brilliant-colored edges of the grains.

OIL PASTELS. You can apply oil pastels to the surface of hardened resin as well as to any media you want to encase in the resin. For the latter, you don't have to dry it first before you pour in your resin. If you apply the oil pastel to hardened resin, you'll need to be sure to let it dry thoroughly. Then add a thin coat of resin on top to preserve and protect the oil pastel.

GLITTER. Glitter adds a rich look to the sides of a metal bezel. All you have to do is coat the metal with a thin layer of resin and sprinkle glitter on it before it dries.

Mixed-Media Layering

When you're mixing media—paper, dried organics such as flowers, metal, and more—you will need to use a "seal-as-you-go" process to keep things in place, that is, adding resin each time you want to affix something in a set place.

SINKING. Use clean stir sticks and/or toothpicks to sink things into your resin. You can also use the toothpicks to pop any remaining bubbles that you don't want.

ADHERING. If you have paper you want to set into the bezel, be sure to adhere it first, rather than putting it in place with all the other materials and pouring in resin. That's because paper is relatively light and will float to the surface. If you are adding several items that are more lightweight, such as dried flowers, you can put everything into a bezel at the same time, then pour in resin; but you'll need to check it every fifteen minutes for the first hour to make sure that nothing has floated to the top. If it has, you can just prod it with a toothpick to set it back where you want it to lie.

Adding Depth & Detail

Once you've assembled your collage and your resin has dried, you can attach additional pieces to your assemblage using a cold join, such as a rivet. When you do this, be sure that if your added piece is metal, you lightly sand the piece and clean it to remove any traces of machine oil before making the attachment.

MATERIALS & TOOLS

4" (10 cm) of 18-gauge round dead-soft wire

5"–6" (12.5–15 cm) of decorative bezel wire

1/16" (2 mm) metal nut-and-screw rivet

Two-part resin, mixing cups, and stir sticks

Toothpicks

Sponge-strip resin applicator

Handheld torch and fuel

Annealing pan and pumice

Fireproof work surface

Heat-resistant tweezers

Quenching pan

1.6 mm metal hole punch

Chasing or ball-peen hammer

Round-nose pliers

Chain-nose pliers

Metal shears

Rubber cement

Clear packing tape

Alcohol wipes

Baby wipes

Nitrile gloves

Large white plastic trash bag

PROJECT:

Decorative-Wire Bezel

Special bezel wire can be purchased from any jewelry-supply store. Originally this product, which is often decoratively stamped, was only made in sterling silver: Alternative metals have recently come onto the market, such as brass, bronze, and copper. In this project, the wire overlaps and is joined with a nut-and-screw rivet. (Your other options for joining would be to solder at the seam in the traditional way or simply bind the triangle together with a wire.)

1 Using the handheld torch, draw a bead on your 18-gauge wire to create a head pin. Quench and set aside. (See page 54.)

2 Form an isosceles triangle (sides will be equal in length and longer than the bottom). First, make a right-angle bend 2" (5 cm) from one end of the bezel wire with chain-nose pliers. Next, make a second right-angle bend 2¼" (5.5 cm) from the first bend. Finally, bend the remaining long piece of bezel wire in the middle, forming a point **(Fig. 1)**. These equal pieces will be the sides of your triangle.

3 Overlap the bezel wire end on the side of the triangle with the short piece of bezel wire on the bottom of the triangle **(Fig. 2)**. (Your overlapping piece should extend down the side no more than an inch [2.5 cm]. Trim if necessary.)

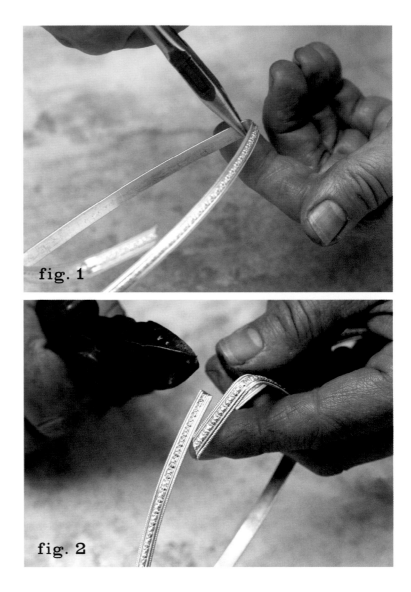

fig. 1

fig. 2

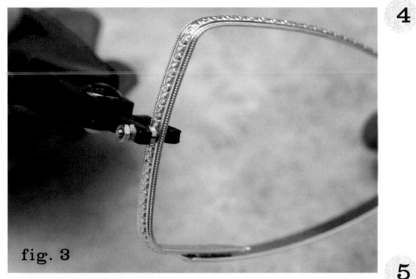

fig. 3

4 Punch a 1/16" (2 mm) hole through both overlapping layers of bezel wire with the hole punch, being careful to keep the wire layers together so the holes align. (You can punch the holes one at a time if that is easier for you, simply measuring and marking to ensure consistency.) Next, punch a hole through the wire that forms the bottom of the triangle (**Fig. 3**).

5 With the short wire piece placed inside the bezel, thread the rivet screw through the aligning holes, starting from the inside of the bezel, nail-head first (**Fig. 4**). Screw the nut onto the shaft, tightening it with chain-nose pliers (**Fig. 5**).

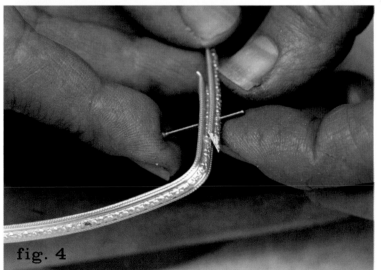

fig. 4

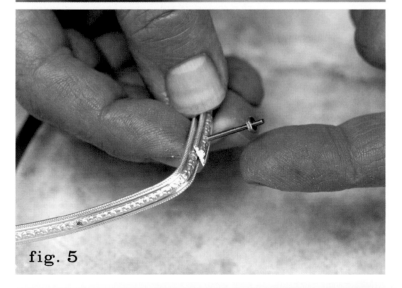

fig. 5

decorative-wire bezel

6 Using metal shears, trim the excess screw shaft, leaving a short remaining piece for creating a nailhead (**Fig. 6**). Strike gently with the round end of the hammer to create the nailhead and a secure riveted connection (**Fig. 7**).

7 Thread the head pin through the hole in the bottom of the triangle, going from the inside to the outside (the balled end will be on the inside) and, using round-nose and chain-nose pliers, make a wrapped loop on the outside of the triangle (**Fig. 8**). Wrap any excess wire around the stem of your loop. It's important to make this tight so that it holds your bezel wire together firmly. Trim the excess wire.

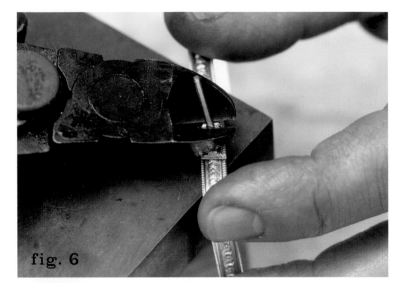
fig. 6

fig. 7

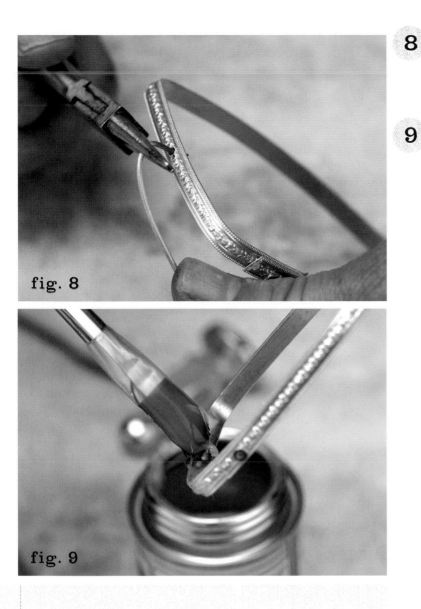

fig. 8

fig. 9

8 Dab rubber cement on the balled end of the wire loop to keep the piece from swiveling when worn **(Fig. 9)**.

9 Place the plastic trash bag on your work surface. Clean the bezel with alcohol wipes and let it dry. Back the bezel with clear packing tape, making sure the tape is smooth and wrinkle-free. (It's important to have clean hands when you do this because any kind of dirt or oily substance will stick to the tape; this will transfer to the resin and will become part of your piece. Even your fingerprints on the tape may leave an impression in the resin.) Add any decorative elements you want to encase in your bezel. Mix and pour your resin to fill. Dome if desired. (See page 24.) Dry for 6 hours.

NOTE
If there is resin leakage, please see page 157 on resin cleanup. You may need to repour.

PROJECT:

Heart
Wire Bezel

MATERIALS & TOOLS

Three 15" (38 cm) pieces of round 16-gauge dead-soft wire

6" (15 cm) piece of 22-gauge dead-soft wire

Paper-collage elements

Two-part resin, mixing cups, and stir sticks

Toothpicks

Sponge-strip resin applicator

Chain-nose pliers

Round-nose pliers

Ball-peen hammer

Bench block or anvil

Scissors

Clear packing tape, wide

Handheld torch and fuel

Annealing pan and pumice

Fireproof work surface

Heat-resistant tweezers

Quenching pan

Bracelet mandrel (optional)

Sharpie permanent marker

Sharp-pointed tool

Large white plastic trash bag

Baby wipes

Nitrile gloves

Alcohol wipes

When I was in art school, using a heart shape to symbolize your work was considered too obvious and trite and was looked down upon. Because of this training, I steered clear of using heart shapes. But a few years ago, many abrupt changes occurred in my life, and I found myself being drawn to and embracing the heart shape and all that it signifies. The hearts I make are typically a bit shaky and dilapidated but, I assure you, this quality is intentional.

1 Using a ball-peen hammer, flatten each piece of the 16-gauge wire on your bench block. Anneal and quench (see page 54).

2 With your torch, draw a bead on both ends of the 22-gauge wire (see page 54). Quench and set this wire aside for later use.

3 Hold your hammered wire lengths together. Grasping the wire layers in the middle with chain-nose pliers, bend the wires in half (**Fig. 1**). This sharp bend at the midpoint creates the bottom tip of your heart form.

4 Form the two rounded portions at the top of the heart. Bend each side with your hands into freeform rounded halves; or you can bend the wire around a bracelet mandrel to achieve uniform halves (**Fig. 2**).

5 After forming the top of your heart, bundle the wires at the center point. Using chain-nose pliers, wrap the 22-gauge wire as tightly as possible around the center wire bundle at the point where the top curves of your heart meet (**Fig. 3**). Trim any excess if desired.

6 Place your wire heart on top of paper with interesting graphics, prints, or handwriting that you want to encase in your bezel. (I used paper that I had precoated with resin to add transparency.) Using a Sharpie marker, trace the bezel outline inside the heart form (**Fig. 4**). Cut out the paper heart and place your wire bezel on top to confirm a good fit.

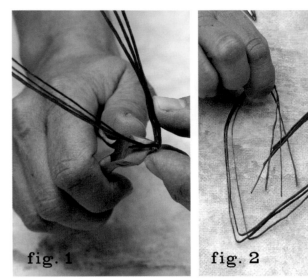

fig. 1

fig. 2

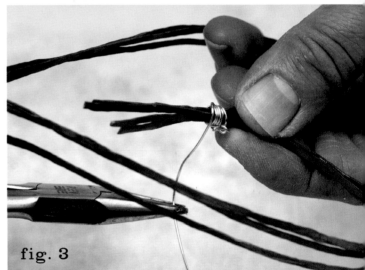

fig. 3

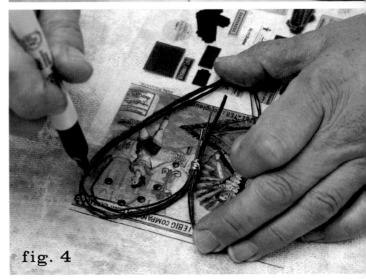

fig. 4

RESIN alchemy

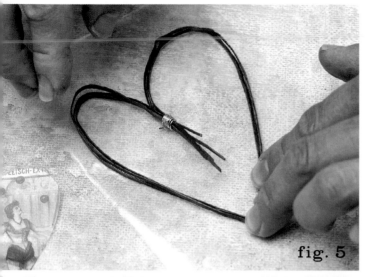

fig. 5

fig. 6

fig. 7

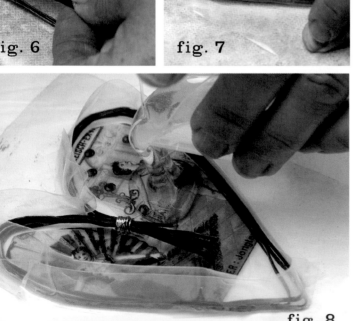

fig. 8

7 Clean the wire heart with alcohol wipes and let it dry. Next, create a back for your open wire bezel. Cut off a piece of clear packing tape large enough to cover the back of your heart, plus a small margin. Lay your piece of packing tape on your worktable, sticky side up. (It's important to have clean hands when you do this because any dirt or oily substances will stick to the tape; this will transfer to the resin and will become part of your piece. Even your fingerprints can leave an impression in the resin.) Press your heart-wire bezel into the tape (**Fig. 5**). Press tightly around the edges to seal the tape completely on the back of your bezel.

8 Carefully place your heart cutout inside the wire bezel onto the tape (**Fig. 6**). Align all edges and make sure this is smoothly nested within—no wrinkles or folds.

9 Cut two or three thin strips of tape and press them onto the outer edges of the heart to form a perpendicular wall that will prevent resin from oozing out of the sides and in between the wires. I like to run a sharp-pointed tool around the bottom edges as an extra measure to seal the sides securely (**Fig. 7**).

10 Place the plastic trash bag on your work surface. Mix and pour the resin into the bezel (**Fig. 8**). When you pour your resin, fragile open-back bezels like this can sometimes leak resin. If there is any resin leakage, please see page 157 on resin cleanup. You may need to repour. Dry for 6 hours.

MATERIALS & TOOLS

Closed-back bezel (premade or found object)

2"–3" (5–7.5 cm) head pin (optional)

4" x 4" (10 x 10 cm) piece of tissue or rice paper for bezel cover

Paper with graphics

2" (5 cm) piece of rhinestone chain

Ephemera: tiny charms, bits of paper with prints or handwriting, small hardware pieces, etc.

Granules: sand, glitter, or any other small objects

Two-part resin, mixing cups, and stir sticks

Toothpicks

Sponge-strip resin applicator

Rubber cement (optional)

Metal hole punch ¹⁄₁₆" (2 mm) diameter

Pencil

Scissors or X-Acto knife

Chain-nose pliers

Round-nose pliers

Needle file

Large white plastic trash bag

Alcohol wipes

Baby wipes

Nitrile gloves

PROJECT:

Shaker-
Box Bezel

My work has always been about movement, which makes this project such a good one. Messages and words, sand from a wonderful beach, or even New Year's confetti can be loosely encased beneath transparent resin-coated paper to shake freely when moved. Whatever you choose to put into your shaker box will spring from your own personal inspiration. This is a great way to use a found-object bezel, such as an empty watchcase. Use your imagination to select bits that tell a story!

1. If your bezel does not have a shank or loop with which to hang your finished piece, you will need to create a loop. To do this, punch a hole where desired and slide a head pin through it; form a simple or wrapped wire loop. Seal with rubber cement if necessary.

2. Place the plastic trash bag on your work surface. Trace the form of the bezel in pencil on an interesting piece of paper with graphics and cut it out. Because I especially like to have a see-through quality in the paper, I choose one I know will be as transparent as possible, such as tissue or rice paper, so I can view the content inside. I do not seal my paper with sealant. Clean the bezel with alcohol wipes and let it dry. Place the paper in the bottom of your bezel. Next, add objects and granules, leaving space within the bezel for them to move and shift freely after the bezel has been sealed (Fig. 1).

fig. 1

fig. 2

3. To seal the bezel, I prefer to use tissue or rice paper because they are the most transparent once they are coated with resin. Lay a small piece of tissue or rice paper over the opening in your bezel so that it overlaps the edges (Fig. 2). Mix the resin and apply it with a small sponge-strip applicator to both sides of the tissue paper, using the trash bag as your work surface.

RESIN alchemy

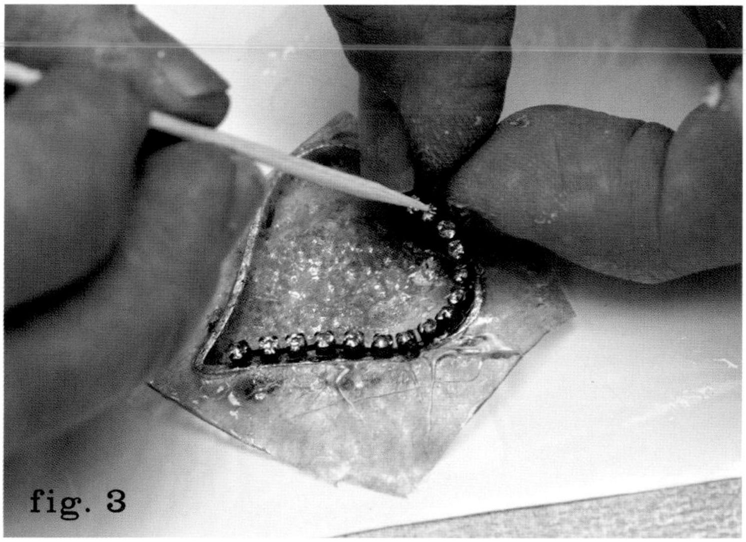

fig. 3

fig. 4

Place the tissue paper over the bezel and gently press around the edges. The resin will both adhere the edges of the paper to the bezel as well as coat the paper surface. Apply resin to the back of the rhinestone chain and place it along the edge of the bezel (**Fig. 3**).

4 Next, cut a small clean piece from the trash bag and place it on top of your resin-coated/rhinestone paper; place a book on top of the trash bag to weight it so that you will achieve a tight seal on your bezel.

5 After 6 hours, when the resin has completely cured, remove the book and peel off the trash bag (it should come off easily). Turn the piece over, top side down, and trim the excess resin paper with the X-Acto knife. Next, using downward strokes, file the edges of your resin paper until smooth and flush with the bezel's edge. Your paper covering should now be a beautiful transparent window that showcases the elements you placed inside the bezel (**Fig. 4**).

WHY I LOVE **ORGANICS:** freestanding resin-coated forms

About six years ago, in a workshop that I was teaching, I spilled resin on some paper. Suddenly I began to see the beautiful transparency that occurred when the paper absorbed resin liquid into its fibers. I realized the possibility of using resin on paper and other objects to achieve two things: **1:** strengthening the paper and giving it plasticity for shaping, and **2:** creating a transparent paper shape. My work was transformed and deeply enriched by this discovery.

Whenever I make a discovery involving a new medium, I like to push the material as far as it will go to unlock all its design possibilities. This whole area of resin exploration began for me with paper, but then expanded into using tree and floral leaves and petals as paper, then preserving sticks, dry foliage, eggshells, lightbulbs, bugs, and anything else that I collected from Mother Nature's garden. Resin was the key to making these materials structurally permanent and fit to be incorporated in jewelry components. Simply put, resin coats, protects, shapes, adheres, and so much more—exactly what fragile materials require to become long-lasting pieces.

In this chapter, you'll learn how to incorporate resin-coated paper and organics into exciting designs: a resin-coated rosebud dangle, resin-coated paper leaves, an eggshell prayer box, and a ring with stacked layers of resin-coated paper.

Paper + Resin

I learned a lot about paper as I experimented with coating many different types of paper with resin. The papers that work best in terms of transparency are rice

Coating actual leaves and torn paper with text with resin creates a wonderful translucency.

paper, silk paper, or any other paper made from plant fibers, such as rag- or linen-based stock. Because the fiber weave in each is porous, the resin can penetrate well to make the paper transparent. In addition to making the paper transparent, the resin strengthens the paper to give it permanency. Pre-1930 French paper and pre-1900 American paper are all made from linen or cotton rag fibers, not wood pulp. You can find these papers in specialty paper stores and online. You can even use delicate tissue paper in your designs by simply coating it heavily with resin.

I have developed various ways to alter and personalize paper. Here are just a few of those effects.

SCAN AND PRINT AN IMAGE OR PHOTO ONTO RICE PAPER. An old love letter from your grandfather to your grandmother, a family picture, any artwork such as sketches or paintings in color or black and white—all of these and more can be used to make unique resin paper components. (When you use images with dark ink, the dense areas of dark ink will not be transparent but will contrast with the lighter transparent areas.)

To create an almost-transparent, faded look with photos, I use a transfer paper normally reserved for fabric. Copy your image onto the transfer paper, using a reverse image setting. (To copy any text, you'll need to reverse it on the printer so it will read correctly; the image will be right side up after it's transferred.) Apply the image to your paper with an iron set on a nonsteam cotton setting. (Follow

Resin is the perfect medium for preserving the beauty of floral petals. Photo by Michelle Monet.

the manufacturer's directions for applying the heat transfer.) The image will transfer quickly, so be ready.

USE A FAVORITE RUBBER STAMP AND STAMP A CLEAR IMAGE WITH PERMANENT INK. Let it dry completely, then coat the paper with resin. (Permanent ink will not run.)

EMBED COLOR AND IMAGERY. Stencil numerals onto the paper with a permanent-ink marker pen such as a Sharpie. (If you use a ballpoint pen, you'll need to heat-set it with an iron so it won't smear when you apply resin.) Sketch some cool images with pencil. Or paint images with oil pastels, acrylic paint, or crayons.

COLOR TORN-EDGED TISSUE. After you have applied resin to tissue and it has dried thoroughly (6 hours), you can rip the now-transparent paper to the size of your project. Next, slowly burn the torn edges to create an aged look. As soon as you've done that, apply some bright oil pastels to the still-warm burned edges. (Normally, oil pastel takes about a year to become permanent, but when applied directly to burned edges, it melts into them and becomes permanent very quickly.) This is one of my favorite techniques: Using it, I built a body of work, called *Letters to My Lover*. I also like to do this to the edges of journal paper.

STRETCH WET RESIN-COATED PAPER ONTO A WIRE FORM OR OVER THE TOP OF A BEZEL. Let it dry to create a hollow, transparent form or bezel cover. Punch holes in dry resin-coated paper and set eyelets to strengthen them. You can now stretch this onto a wire frame to make a journal cover.

TEXTURE PAPER. There are several ways to texture paper before you apply resin. You can emboss paper using a paper-rolling mill (Grand Caliber is a good one) to create a variety of patterns, imprints, and cutouts. You can also score the paper with a dull-edged knife to give it interesting lines. Or use a burnishing tool to rub the paper over a raised surface with a pattern (a texture plate works well).

Organics + Resin

Here's a short list of some of the organic things to which you can apply resin to create interesting components: dried flowers, bugs, feathers, dry or wet leaves, twigs,

I press natural flowers in a book and dry them before encasing them in resin. Photo by Michelle Monet.

and eggshells. Before you apply resin to these organic materials, think about how you might alter the surface of the material beforehand. For instance, a stick or branch can be etched using a wood-burning tool or carved with graffiti using an awl or another sharply pointed tool. You can then rub oil pastel color into these recesses to accent and add depth to them. Or you can draw images, letters, numerals, and words with a permanent-ink pen on the surface of leaves or eggshells, then seal them with resin.

Once you've discovered the effects you like best, you can create freestanding forms to enhance any number of jewelry and art pieces. (Be bold when you experiment with effects and try anything you can imagine—simply discard what doesn't work or figure out how to make it work.) Even though resin is a very flexible and forgiving medium to work with, you'll want to consider following these tips to ensure the very best results each time you work with it.

A Few Tips for Success

PROTECTING YOUR SKIN. When working with resin, you can protect your skin from absorbing it by wearing nitrile gloves (available at the drugstore or in craft stores) or by coating your hands in mineral lotion. This protection will become more

Make nature-infused works with resin-coated feathers, leaves, flower buds, shells, and sticks.

For delicate organics, I spread a thin coat of resin on them gently.

Coat a twig by dipping it into resin.

why i love organics

Dry your resin-dipped twig on the surface of a plastic garbage bag.

Strengthen a weak stem by wrapping it in waxed linen thread and coating with resin.

important to you as you increase your output of resin-coated materials.

APPLYING RESIN. I often dip organic materials, such as twigs, directly into my resin to ensure that they will be heavily coated. However, I opt for an alternative application method for other, more delicate materials, such as feathers or flower petals. On these, I spread a thin coat of resin onto the surface. Inexpensive kitchen sponges, cut into very small strips or squares, are ideal tools for this alternative technique. Because the sponges are absorbent, they minimize resin drip as you apply the resin, giving you more control over the thickness of your coating. They're also a good tool for pushing resin into crevices and small spaces that you want to fill.

DRYING. The best drying surface I have found for my resin-coated materials is a large white plastic trash bag. It's the only plastic that can be pried easily from the surface of a resin-coated object. As soon as your resin-coated paper or organics are dry, just grasp a corner of your material and pull it away gently from the surface of the plastic bag.

When you dip a component in resin, make sure to check your piece fifteen minutes after you've set it down to dry, then move it to another place to finish drying. This will help you avoid ending up with a pool of unwanted resin attached to the piece after it is dry. It is much more work to clip off the dried excess and sand the piece than it is to take this simple step.

PRESTRENGTHENING ORGANICS. When I coat an organic, such as a flower bud, with resin, the bud may have a weak, dry stem that I want to retain for attachment. If this is the case, I strengthen the stem by first wrapping it with a waxed linen thread or string. Then I coat the stem—string and

When dried flowers protrude from a bezel, coat them with resin to strengthen.

Metal backing on the lip of this eggshell gives it strong "bones."

all—in resin. After the wrapped stem has dried, I can drill through it without worrying that it will break. For organic materials that will protrude from a component (say, flowers set in a bezel), I coat the materials with resin and dry them, then add them to my bezel afterward. Using this two-step approach, my piece looks its best—no sloppy overflow or unexpected surprises.

ATTACHING. When adding fragile, free-form objects to a design that will have movement (such as dangles), I attach them with a cold join. This is the strongest jewelry engineering technique you can use and ensures that your component connection will not break when it's bumped.

BACKING. I always back or frame fragile components with metal to provide good structural "bones," and because it simply looks more beautiful to me.

Resin
Hollow Forms

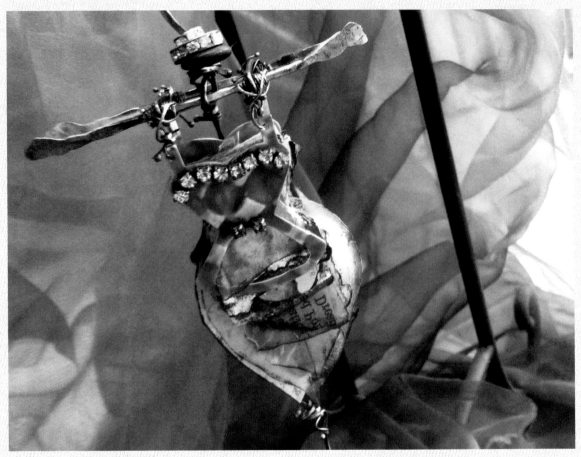

A wire cage wrapped in resin-coated paper offers a window to intriguing contents.

I like movement in my pieces and have used cold joins and mixed-media materials to create this. Because I'm always looking for new ways to make kinetic objects, I found a fabulous way to create hollow forms that move and shake. These containers can hold anything from shredded dollar bills to flashing glitter (best to avoid using objects that are too sharp). Oftentimes, I seal in a note or message meant only for me. These miniature hollow worlds draw the viewer in deep. Inside is an artistic "ecosystem" that is ever-changing.

Here are examples of two techniques that will help you create your own small resin worlds:

1 MAKE A COVERED FORM. This can be as simple as covering tiny lightbulbs with resin. After the resin has been applied to the exterior of the form, you simply cut an opening in the top with an X-Acto knife and pull out the interior wiring with pliers. Next, use a tiny brush to coat the interior with resin for extra strengthening. Ideas for things to place inside your newly created resin form are seeds; beach sand; tiny strips of paper with letters, numbers, and messages; sticks; feathers; and glitter. These are all materials that can both signify meaning and move freely inside your hollow form.

2 SEAL A BEZEL WITH RESIN-COATED PAPER. Tissue paper and rice paper are my favorites for this technique because of their transparency once resin has been applied. For a bezel form with a back (could be metal or simply an acorn or a pod that's been sliced open), cut a piece of paper that is slightly larger than the bezel. Fill the bezel with your choice of materials. (If you use an organic bezel, you will have to seal it first with a sealant.) Then coat the paper with resin on both sides and place it on top of the bezel opening. Next, seal it by placing a plastic bag on the resin paper, then a book to weight it down while it dries. For an open-back bezel, you'll simply create a backing with resined pa-

Encasing glitter, shredded dollar bills, and tiny "secret" notes in your hollow form creates small worlds.

per and let it dry. Add your materials and place resin-coated paper on top as with the closed-bezel form. (See project on page 86.)

If you want to give the top of your sealed bezel a filmy, layered look, just add more layers of resin paper to your bezel.

Embedding Images in Resin: Heat Transfers

Embedding images and messages on paper through heat transfer, then coating the paper with resin, makes resin's transparency totally expressive—and preserves these visuals. I have come up with as many options as possible so that any artist can create personalized designs. Using heat-transfer techniques, I incorporate a lot of printed and handwritten text, photographs, and print images. If you are a painter or sketch artist, there are techniques to transfer your work onto tissue paper, to which you then apply resin for transparency or translucency. You can use such things as handwriting from old letters, pencil sketches, photographs, or stamped images (from premade rubber or wood stamps or from your own custom designs). Maybe you want to preserve your grandfather's signature, or some childhood vacation photos, or even a line of poetry printed in an antique book. Or perhaps you want to incorporate some small paintings or crayon drawings or even watercolors. Unleash your imagination to discover unique possibilities.

Stamped or photocopied images are great transfer options.

HEAT TRANSFERS. I use heat transfers to incorporate images into my resin designs. Techni-Print 4.0 is my top choice because I can use either an ink-jet or a laser printer with it. Also, the negative spaces in my images remain transparent after they are heat-transferred to paper. Rice paper is my top pick of paper because I like its texture and transparency. I'm also able to transfer an image to a fabric that is either a loose weave and/or thin, such as gauze: I simply bind it by covering it with a thin sheet of plastic before I press on the transfer using an iron that is on a nonsteam cotton setting.

Use a nonsteam setting on your iron to press on your transfer.

Layer handwriting with art and transparent and opaque papers for depth.

COPYING ORIGINAL IMAGES. For any visual that you want to photocopy in order to preserve the original, remember that when you transfer the image, it'll be a mirror image. Handwriting is the most obvious visual that needs to be reversed when it's copied in order to transfer properly. For digital images, you can print directly from your computer onto transfer paper.

TRANSFERABLE MEDIA. You can make your own art to embed using heat transfers. The range of possibilities is huge: permanent markers, rubber stamps with permanent ink, any oil-based paints, crayons, graphite and colored pencils, even watercolors. The only extra step you need to take when you have a water-based ink or paint is to heat-set the ink by pressing it with an iron on a nonsteam setting.

LAYERING IMAGES. If you want to create a look of depth and mystery when combining several images—say, a photo and some handwriting—apply the transfers in layers. You can add even more depth by layering with both transparent and opaque papers. Achieving opacity or translucency depends on the paper quality. More fragile papers, such as tissue paper, become completely transparent when resin is applied, while sturdier linen or cotton rag paper stock will be more opaque. If you have a paper with a glossy finish that has an image you plan to transfer, just be sure to lightly sand the finish first so the transfer will adhere.

PROJECT:

Resin-coated
Rosebuds

MATERIALS & TOOLS

Dried rosebuds with stems

Two-part resin, mixing cups, and stir sticks

Linen twine or string

Scissors

Sticky wax

Handheld or electric drill, with 1/16" (2 mm) drill bit

Metal file

Metal end cap (optional)

Large white plastic trash bag

Alcohol wipes

Baby wipes

Nitrile gloves

On my first trip to southern France, twelve jewelry-making students and I visited Paris first to absorb some of that city's famed culture. Paris overflows with femininity—stylish perfume bottles, handmade lace trim, and beautiful fresh-cut and dried flowers. Soon, I found myself using pink as a predominant color in my work: I still have not recovered! The resin-coated rosebuds that I often use in my designs stem from this powerful experience in the city of love.

1 Place the plastic trash bag on your work surface. Wrap twine around the stem of the rosebud several times (**Fig. 1**); tie firmly and trim the twine and bud ends closely with scissors (**Fig. 2**).

2 Mix the resin. Dip a rosebud, string and all, into the resin and lay it on top of the trash bag (**Fig. 3**). Repeat with the remaining rosebuds. After 15 minutes, the excess liquid resin will have pooled under your flower buds. Wear nitrile gloves to pick up the flowers by the stem (**Fig. 4**). Transfer them to a clean spot on the plastic bag to finish drying completely.

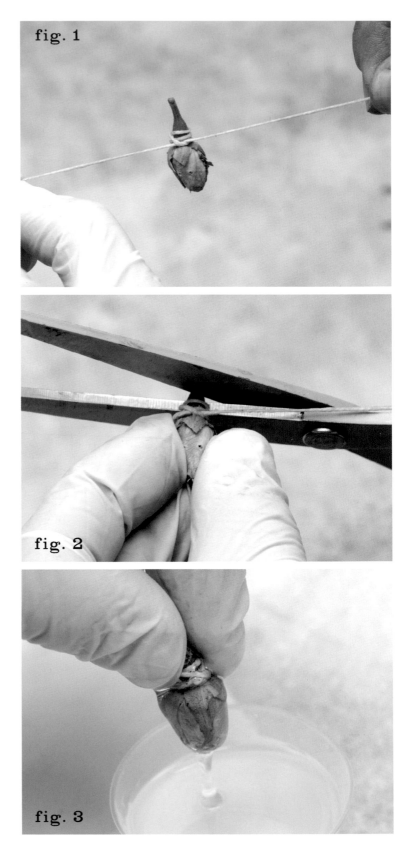

fig. 1

fig. 2

fig. 3

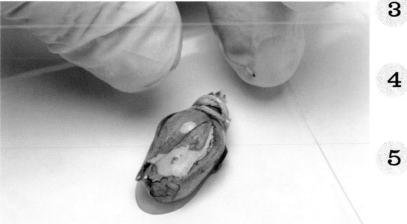

fig. 4

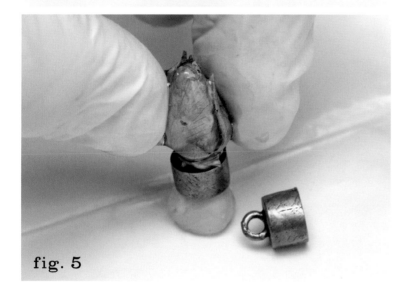

fig. 5

3 After your flowers are dry, file and clean up any excess dried resin around the buds.

4 Gently drill through the string-wrapped stem to create a hole for connection.

5 Alternatively, you can glue an end cap on the end of the string if you'd like to hide it. First, clean the end cap with alcohol wipes and let it dry. Next, insert the end cap into a small pea-sized lump of sticky wax, open end up **(Fig. 5)**. Then, apply resin to the inside of the cap; insert the rosebud stem and let it dry.

MATERIALS & TOOLS

Thirteen 7" (18 cm) pieces of 16-gauge half-hard wire

Rice or tissue paper

Permanent-ink pen

Oil pastels

Two-part resin, mixing cups, and stir sticks

Sponge-strip applicator

Ball-peen hammer

Bench block or anvil

Handheld torch and fuel (optional)

Annealing pan and pumice (optional)

Fireproof work surface (optional)

Quenching pan (optional)

Heat-resistant tweezers (optional)

Chain-nose pliers

Round-nose pliers

Wire cutters

X-Acto knife

Metal file

Large white plastic trash bag

Baby wipes

Nitrile gloves

PROJECT:

Resin-coated Paper Leaves

Because I am a jeweler at heart, once I began coating paper with resin, I immediately set out to explore ways to give my paper structural support with metal. As I worked on an idea for resin-coated leaves made of paper, I sought to create a very fragile and feminine look. While you can make any leaf shape you desire, I chose an oval for this project. I think this simple technique with a wire frame hits the mark.

1 Hammer your 16-gauge wire pieces flat on a bench block. Using outward strokes, flare the ends of your wire pieces with the flat end of your hammer **(Fig. 1)**.

2 Using chain-nose pliers, grasp the wire at a point one-third of the way down the wire's length; bend it into a sharp V **(Fig. 2)**. (Your wire will be work-hardened after flattening. If it feels stiff, anneal it before bending.)

3 Use your hands to shape the wire into an oval. Wire-wrap the shorter end of the wire around the longer end to close the oval **(Fig. 3)**. Trim the short end flush.

4 Form a wire-wrapped loop on the open end of your long wire **(Fig. 4)**. Repeat Steps 2–4 for the remaining 12 pieces of wire.

5 Place a piece of thin paper (tissue or rice paper is best) onto a cutting surface. Position the wire leaf shape on top and use the outer edge as a guide to cut the paper with an X-Acto knife: It should overlap all edges of the wire **(Fig. 5)**.

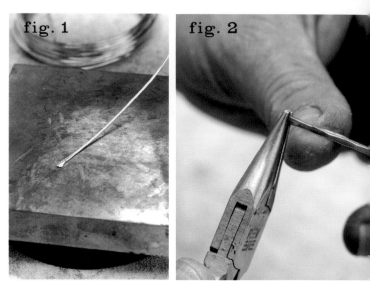

fig. 1   fig. 2

fig. 3

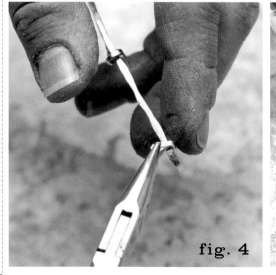

fig. 4   fig. 5

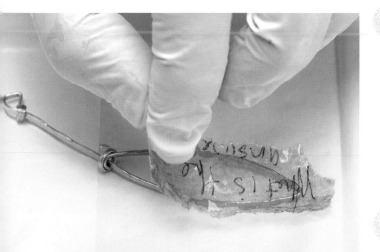

fig. 6

6 Place the plastic trash bag on your work surface. Mix the resin. Using a sponge-strip applicator, apply the resin onto both sides of the paper, using the trash bag as both a work and drying surface. Place the wet resined paper on the wire leaf, pressing gently around the edges (**Fig. 6**). Repeat Steps 5–6 for the remaining 12 pieces of wire. Let the paper leaves dry for 6 hours; trim the excess paper with the X-Acto knife and/or file.

7 To add definition and color to the leaves, rub the tip of a permanent-ink pen along the edges of the resin (**Fig. 7**). When you're done, add oil pastel color to the edges.

8 You can now use finished leaves in any arrangement you desire. They can be dangles that hang loosely from a piece of wire, or they can be joined by wire in a daisy-chain fashion (**Fig. 8**). It's your choice!

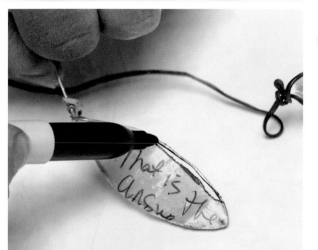

fig. 7

fig. 8

NOTE
If you wish to add a patina to your wire, dip it into liver of sulfur before you apply the paper and resin.

resin-coated paper leaves

Two 6" (15 cm) pieces of 18-gauge half-hard wire

One 3" (7.5 cm) piece of 18-gauge half-hard wire

One 2" (5 cm) piece of 8- or 10-gauge dead-soft wire

Two open-ended metal bezels (found-objects or purchased)

Two small metal washers or bead spacers

One-half of a small eggshell*

One small piece of decorative paper

Two-part resin, mixing cups, and stir sticks

Small plastic cup

Sponge-strip applicator

Round-nose pliers

Flat-nose pliers

Ball-peen hammer

Bench block or anvil

Metal hole punch, 1/16" (2 mm) diameter

Handheld torch and fuel

Annealing pan and pumice

Fireproof work surface

Heat-resistant tweezers

Quenching pan

Sharpie permanent marker

Fine-grit sandpaper

Large white plastic trash bag

Alcohol wipes

Baby wipes

Nitrile gloves

*You can use a found egg (only if it has been abandoned) or purchase fresh quail eggs at most Asian markets.

PROJECT:

Eggshell
Prayer Box

As an artist, I spend a lot of time in nature, where I find peace and study nature's organic forms. I like to bring these shapes into my art whenever I can. Once, on a walk with my kids, we discovered a small robin's egg that the tiny bird had left behind on the ground. I immediately saw how perfect its small, cupped shape would be for a bezel. In fact, the shape of this tiny egg was similar to that of many prayer boxes from India that I had collected in my travels. Once you have created your own Eggshell Prayer Box, store an object or note in it that holds special meaning for you.

1 Gently crack your egg in half, drain the contents, and let the shell halves dry.

2 Place the trash bag on your work surface. Clean one of the bezels with alcohol wipes and let it dry. Coat one eggshell half with resin inside and out. To ensure that the eggshell is very durable, apply multiple coats, drying between each. After it has completely dried, attach the eggshell to the bezel by setting the broken edge of the shell over the bezel opening. Where the eggshell makes contact with the surface of the metal bezel, the resin will act as glue to adhere the two surfaces. (Coat the other half-shell with resin, dry, and save for a future project.) Dry for 6 hours; if excess resin drips from the shell, refer to Chapter 7 (page 156) for finishing techniques.

3 Clean the second bezel with alcohol wipes and let it dry. Spread a thin coat of resin onto both sides of a small piece of paper with a sponge-strip applicator, using the trash bag as your work surface. Place the wet resined paper over the open end of your second bezel, pressing the edges gently. Dry for 6 hours.

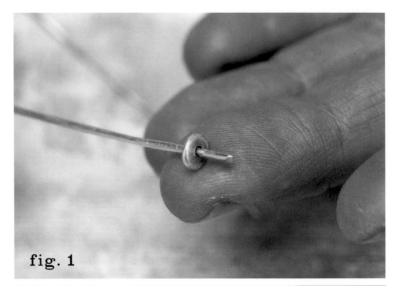

fig. 1

fig. 2

RESIN alchemy

fig. 3

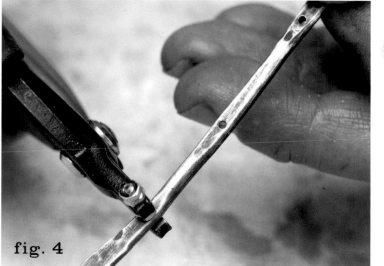

fig. 4

4 At the bottom of each 6" (15 cm) piece of 18-gauge wire, form a loop with round-nose pliers, then slide a washer or bead spacer onto the wire (**Fig. 1**).

5 Thread the unlooped ends of your wire pieces through the holes on each side of your bezel, starting with the side that has the attached eggshell (**Fig. 2**).

6 Thread your second bezel onto the unlooped ends of the wire so that it forms a lid over the eggshell bezel half (**Fig. 3**).

7 Hammer the 2" (5 cm) piece of wire flat. Mark one dot in the center of the wire, then two equidistant marks on either side of that. Using the metal hole punch, punch three holes into the wire (**Fig. 4**).

eggshell prayer box

8 Slide the two wires from your prayer box into the two outside holes on the flat wire, making sure that the wire ends extend equally beyond the holes (**Fig. 5**).

9 Turn your component, eggshell end up, and grasp the middle of the flat-wire piece with flat-nose pliers. With your free hand, use the handheld torch to form a ball at each wire end (**Fig. 6**). (See page 54 for instructions on drawing a ball on wire.)

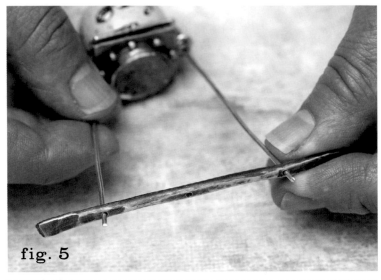

fig. 5

fig. 6

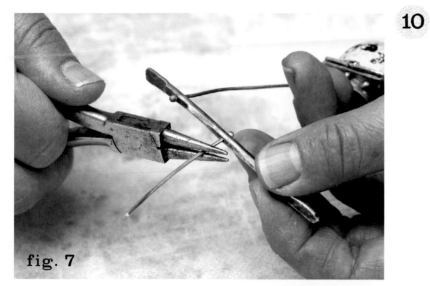

fig. 7

10 Next, use your torch to form a ball at one end of your remaining short piece of 18-gauge wire. Quench. Thread the unballed end through the center hole in the flat wire piece and form a wire-wrapped loop on the top, using round-nose pliers (**Fig. 7**). This loop is the attachment that will connect it to a necklace or another assemblage (**Fig. 8**).

fig. 8

PROJECT:

Resin-coated
Stacked
Paper Ring

MATERIALS & TOOLS

One 12" (30.5 cm) piece of 16-gauge half-hard wire

Four to six small metal washers or spacer beads

Resin-coated papers (clear and with print or writing)

Metal disc for ring base

Permanent-ink pad

Oil pastels

Paper-hole punch

Handheld torch and fuel

Annealing pan and pumice

Fireproof work surface

Heat-resistant tweezers

Quenching pan

Handheld or electric drill with ¹⁄₁₆" (2 mm) drill bit

Hammer

Bench block or anvil

Ring mandrel

Chain-nose pliers

I love the look of the rough and raw edges of burned and colored resin-coated papers that are piled in a stack. I often use dictionary paper of all kinds to create these and even write my own words on tissue to create layers of embedded talismans. The look is fabulous and colorful. The layers of coated paper can be stacked high as a ring or flipped in the other direction as a tassel.

1. Rip resin-coated paper into small circular or square pieces about 1" (2.5 cm) wide (about eight to ten pieces).

2. Ink the edges of your resin papers and/or rub oil pastels on them for color (Fig. 1).

3. Use a paper punch to place a hole in the center of each piece of paper (Fig. 2).

4. Using your torch, create a ball at one end of the wire. Quench. Thread a washer next to the ball end (Fig. 3).

5. Begin threading punched papers onto your wire. Add about three or four sheets of small paper pieces; then add another washer for height, until you reach the height you prefer, ending with a washer on top (Fig. 4). Set aside.

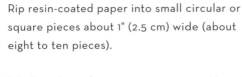

fig. 1

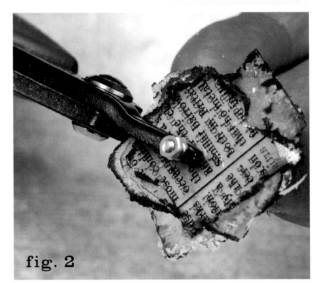

fig. 2

fig. 3

fig. 4

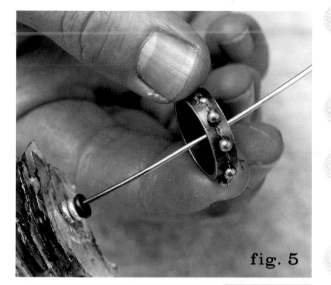

fig. 5

6 Drill a hole in the center of your metal disc. The disc will be used as the base of your ring to support the stacked papers. Thread the disc onto the wire (Fig. 5).

7 If desired, hammer the free end of the wire to flatten (Fig. 6).

8 Place the underside of the metal disc next to a ring mandrel on the mark that signifies your ring size. Wind the free end of the wire around the mandrel at least three times (Fig. 7).

9 Once the wire is almost used up, wrap the end of the wire with chain-nose pliers underneath your metal disc to fasten it well (Fig. 8).

fig. 6

fig. 8

fig. 7

resin-coated stacked paper ring

FORMFITTING
DESIGNS:
casting resin

My interest in resin began many years ago. I have always had a passion for incorporating transparency in my work. Back in the 1990s, I used to travel to Thailand to buy as many tiny handmade transparent beads as I could transport home. I loved the way the dirt from many years of wear had wedged its way beneath the edges of these old glass beads to give them an ancient appearance. Each one looked like a relic that had been treasured by a family or tribe for generations. This look of wear was something I wanted to replicate in my own work.

To re-create the look of antiquity in my own work, I sand down the edges of resin forms and rub gilder's paste or brown acrylic paint into all the sanded edges, cracks, and textures. This process creates a rich, natural-looking patina on the surface of resin forms.

In my figurative work, resin has allowed me to create forms that look like they are glass. When I first began creating a series of jointed circus figures that had removable and wearable jewelry, I tried to use glass to make them. However, I soon found that glass was limiting for me in terms of the surface treatments I could apply and the degree to which I could manipulate the material.

Resin: A Perfect Casting Medium

I turned next to casting in resin and a whole new world of possibilities opened up to me. As with any medium I use, I wanted to push the envelope with resin. I found I could incorporate many different inclusions and colors—liquid or powder, hot or cold. I explored what I liked and didn't like as I experimented with both interior work and exterior surface applications. I discovered that I could cast resin in an open mold, creating a hollowed form into which I could place decorative ingredients, such as paper and tiny objects, exactly where I wanted them to be. By creating a matching open mold, I could make a sealed hollow form, using resin to glue the two pieces together seamlessly.

I also experimented with drying cast pieces at a cool temperature until they were only about 75 percent dry. This allowed me to stretch and manipulate the pieces into different shapes, taking the elasticity of resin to its limits. When a medium has as many applications and dimensions as resin does, it also stretches an artist's creativity.

As you will learn in this chapter, the point at which you pull your cast resin from its mold is just the beginning of the process. The real artwork begins as you transform this flat, uninteresting piece into a beautiful, lightweight jewelry component. The surface treatments and shaping you apply to resin, together with color and found objects, will make each piece uniquely yours.

First Steps First: Making a Mold

CREATING A NEGATIVE MOLD

You can build a mold with many different materials, ranging from plaster and papier-mâché to rubber silicone putty from the hardware store. Some materials are difficult to work with, while others are super-simple. Unless I am planning to cast a very large piece, I prefer to use two-part silicone molding putty.

My favorite mold material, which I use 99 percent of the time, is a nontoxic two-part silicone molding putty. It picks up fine details in an object. Also, when you mix the two parts together, all bubbles vanish, to give you an especially smooth negative of your object. (This is the mold material I have worked with in this book.)

If you aren't ready to make your own finished molds, you can buy ready-made molds from chocolate stores, candy-making supply stores, and craft stores. Some can be very interesting and, by changing the other materials you use with your resin, you can really make a distinctive piece.

Two-Part Silicone Molding Putty

In addition to being exceedingly smooth and capable of picking up extremely fine details, two-part silicone molding putty is also well lubricated. Because of this, you will not have to use a mold release for the first few resin castings. When you begin to have trouble releasing your finished resin castings, coat the inside of your mold with a mold release available in craft stores or a very thin coating of oil (such as olive oil).

To combine, hold equal amounts of each part of the silicone putty in your hands and knead very briskly on a flat surface. (Mixing the two-part silicone putty differs from mixing two-part liquid resin in that you do not have to be so precise in your measuring.)

Once you begin the blending process, you have about five minutes before the silicone putty sets up. Within two minutes, the putty begins to harden and may soon resist the object that you are trying to cast—so it's important to work very quickly. On your work surface, form the blended silicone putty into a ball, making sure that the ball is as large as the object that you want to cast.

First hold equal parts of silicone putty.

Knead the two parts of putty until well combined.

The kneaded ball of putty is now ready for creating a mold.

For an Open Negative Mold

Press the object you wish to cast front first into the silicone putty. Make sure to build up the walls of the putty around your object to avoid resin leakage. I use open molds quite often. They are especially good for helping you control the placement and layering of objects into your resin. When I work on faces for my figurative pieces, I pour the lips first, then the cheeks, then the head (with a word placed into it), etc.

For a Closed Negative Mold

When I am imagining a dimensional piece, I use a closed mold. A closed mold is also my pick when I focus on a single color or texture inside the mold. Starting at the bottom of your object, completely encase it in silicone putty, leaving a small opening at the top of your piece from which you'll remove the object.

After your mold dries in five minutes, you can extract from it the object you encased. With a closed mold, you may have to cut open the side of your mold with scissors or a jeweler's saw. This opening will create no problems at all when you pour in resin later; simply place a rubber band around your mold to hold the cut seams together completely.

If you pour in resin immediately after creating the mold, consider your first pour a throwaway (just as with pancakes!). At this early stage, the mold is outgassing, which creates tiny bubbles in your resin. You can avoid bubbling by heating your mold at 90–135°F (32–57°C) for an hour

This ballerina's head is a closed negative mold in which I intentionally encased bubbles for textural effect. Photo by Michelle Monet.

in the toaster oven or dehydrator. Sometimes, however, I like to incorporate these bubbles into my finished piece intentionally. It can be a fun special effect.

For a Positive Mold

Think of your mold as a simple bezel and pour resin into it following the instructions in Chapter 1 (see page 26). When you pour your resin, think about how useful it may be to insert a metal wire that protrudes beyond the resin to use as an attachment, especially for moving parts. I always add these protrusions to my figurative pieces— especially for movable arms and legs. You can also add springs and wire to use as a hanger for the finished piece. A final choice you can make is whether to pour resin in layers or all at one time. Resin layers give depth and dimension if you embed something in each one (such as paper strips, glitter, a tiny charm), while pouring all your resin at once gives the piece the look of clarity and solidity.

Finishing Touches in Resin

Once you've pulled your resin piece from the mold, it's time for cleanup, filing, sanding, and other surface work. The finishing work on your project will raise the quality of your finished piece to a much finer level. (See Chapter 7, "Finishes and Fixes.")

The small resin figure encased in metal is an example of a closed negative mold.

Negative Mold
Open Form

MATERIALS & TOOLS

Two-part resin, mixing cups, and stir sticks

Toothpicks

Two-part silicone molding putty

Bronze or silver mica powder

Vintage-looking lock or similar metal object

Rhinestone chain (about 1½" [3.8 cm])

Acrylic paint

Needle file

Fine-tipped paintbrush

Metal shears

Large white plastic trash bag

Baby wipes

Nitrile gloves

I love the look of vintage hardware and ancient relics. Whenever I visit Paris, I scour its flea markets and invariably find beautiful worn and weathered vintage hardware. You can simulate that vintage look by adding mica powders to resin. A bonus is that, although mica is entirely composed of stone and metal, it weighs far less than metal. Mica comes in a few different colors, such as bronze, silver, and copper. To make this vintage lock, I used bronze.

1. Place the plastic trash bag on your work surface. Using a two-part silicone molding putty (you want to use a good one that picks up fine details), mix and knead equal parts together in your hands quickly. (You have about 2 minutes to combine. If you wait too long, your silicone putty will harden and resist the object you are molding.)

2. Form your silicone putty into a ball, place it on your work surface, and shape it into roughly the same shape as the lock you are encasing (**Fig. 1**).

3. Gently and firmly press the lock into the putty. Next, build up the sides of your putty to make sure that you have good walls that will prevent the resin from leaking out (**Fig. 2**).

4. Dry the putty mold for 5 minutes. Now, gently separate the lock from the mold and push it out (**Fig. 3**).

5. Fill an empty resin mixing cup three-quarters full with mica powder. Set aside. Mix the resin and pour it into the cup filled with mica powder. Stir well to blend thoroughly and pour carefully into your hardware mold (**Fig. 4**). Dry for 6 hours.

fig. 1

fig. 2

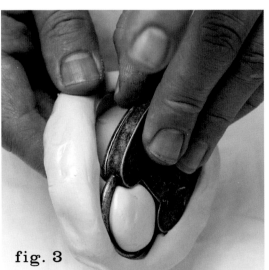

fig. 3

fig. 4

RESIN alchemy

fig. 5

fig. 6

6 Carefully peel the mold away from the resin lock (**Fig. 5**).

7 Smooth the rough outer edges of the resin lock with a needle file. If the edges of your piece have some large resin overflow, use metal shears to trim the excess close to the outer edges of the lock (**Fig. 6**). Repeat filing and trimming cleanup on the inside edge of the lock.

8 Using a small paintbrush, apply acrylic color (I've used blue here) to the recessed keyhole in the lock (**Fig. 7**).

9 Cut the piece of rhinestone chain to fit the length of the lock handle. Embellish the handle by gluing the chain onto it with resin (**Fig. 8**).

fig. 7   fig. 8

negative mold open form

Negative Mold
Closed Form

MATERIALS & TOOLS

- Two-part silicone molding putty
- Two-part resin, mixing cups, and stir sticks
- Toothpicks
- Small dimensional object
- Acrylic paints (optional)
- Bronze gilder's paste (optional)
- Mica or glitter (optional)
- Rhinestones (optional)
- Rubber bands (optional)
- Paper towel
- Scissors or jeweler's saw (optional)
- Needle file
- Sandpaper
- Metal shears
- Large white plastic trash bag
- Baby wipes
- Nitrile gloves

Closed molds are ideal for casting dimensional objects—a small figure; body parts such as legs, arms, a head (if you are not pouring in layers); shells; and any other object that must have a dimensional front and back. I often add paint, mica, or glitter to the resin I pour into these. After the pieces dry, I sand and rub a patina paint into them. That done, they look beautifully finished!

1. Using a two-part silicone molding putty, mix and knead equal parts together in your hands quickly to form a shape close in size to your object (**Fig. 1**).

2. Encase your dimensional object by inserting it into the putty. Manipulate the putty until it completely surrounds the object. Leave a small opening in the mold where you inserted your object.

3. Flatten the bottom of the mold (the end without the opening) with the piece inside (**Fig. 2**): When you pour in resin, you'll have a nice level mold. Let your mold dry for 5 minutes.

4. Push your object out of the mold. It may be difficult to push it out of the small opening, but silicone is very flexible. However, if you are unable to push out the object, you can cut down one side of the mold with scissors or a jeweler's saw. If you have to cut the side, simply align the cut edges and place a rubber band or two around the outside of the mold to keep it sealed.

fig. 1

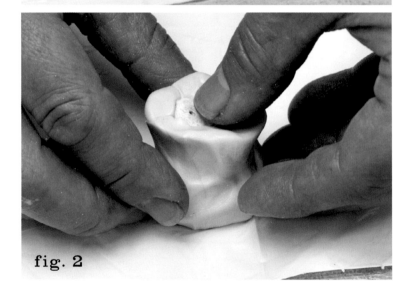

fig. 2

fig. 3

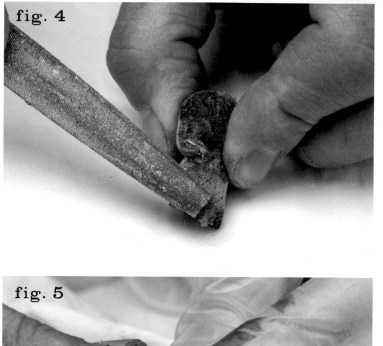

fig. 4

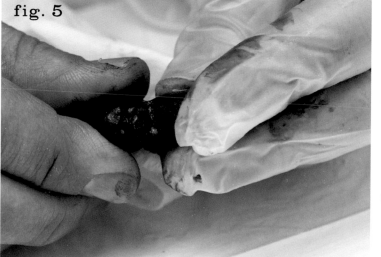

fig. 5

5 Place the plastic trash bag on your work surface. Mix the resin. To add color, dip the end of a clean stir stick that has a drop of acrylic paint on it into the resin and stir. If you want a more intense color, just add additional drops and stir until you have the coloration you want. Alternatively, you can stir glitter or mica into your resin.

6 Because your mold is almost closed, it is hard for air to escape. Fill resin halfway and push out air pockets with a toothpick or clean stir stick (**Fig. 3**). Finish filling and once more poke out air pockets. Dry for 6 hours.

7 Pull your piece out of the mold. File and/or sand any rough edges and clip off the excess resin with metal shears (**Fig. 4**).

8 To add patina to the piece and give it highlights, rub either brown acrylic paint or antique bronze gilder's paste into the piece (**Fig. 5**). Rub away the excess with a paper towel.

9 At this point, you can add a secondary color for depth and/or embellish the piece by gluing on rhinestones.

TECHNIQUE:

Resin
Druzy
Stones

MATERIALS & TOOLS

Two-part silicone molding putty

Two-part resin, mixing cups, and stir sticks

Toothpicks

White and black oil paints

Forms to create negative molds (various simple shapes)

Glass glitter,* coarse or fine

Large white plastic trash bag

Baby wipes

Nitrile gloves

*Note: I do like the better quality and look of glass glitter. But not always: With cold enameling, I use a very light, fine synthetic glitter because it blends better into the enamel.

I use crystal geodes and druzy stones a lot in my metalworking because I like their beautiful glittery surfaces. They're used in many of the big, bold rings I have made. It occurred to me that it would be easy to re-create the look of these stones in resin by simply embedding glass glitter or glass frit (ground glass). Resin druzy stones are easy to make, and they look just like the real thing!

1. Place the plastic trash bag on your work surface. Knead the two-part silicone molding putty, using equal portions of both parts, until well blended. Create several open negative molds by pressing various shapes into the putty—circles, rectangles, triangles, any simple shapes. The sides of these molds should be about ½" (1.3 cm) high. Nontoxic rubber silicone molding material takes about 10 minutes to dry **(Fig. 1)**.

2. Mix the resin. Next, using a clean stir stick, add a drop each of white and black oil paints. Stir until the resin is gray (to simulate the look of stone) **(Fig. 2)**.

3. Pour the resin into the molds until each is half full. A clean stir stick is a useful tool for drizzling the resin into these small molds and spreading it evenly **(Fig. 3)**. Dry for 6 hours.

4. Mix and apply a thin layer of clear resin to the surface of each resin mold using a clean stir stick to spread evenly **(Fig. 4)**.

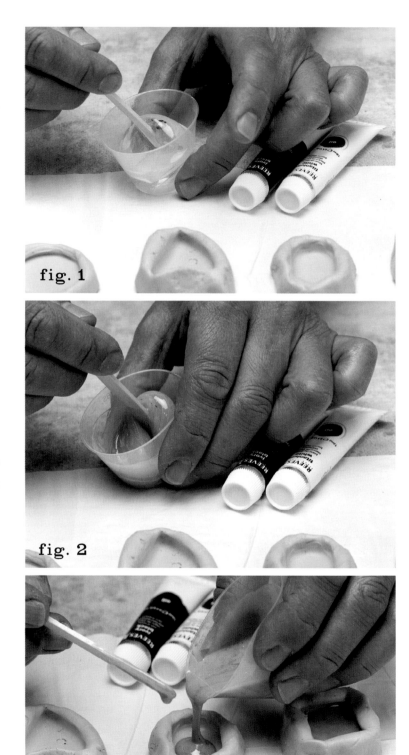

fig. 1

fig. 2

fig. 3

RESIN alchemy

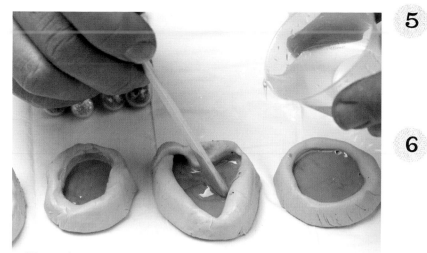

fig. 4

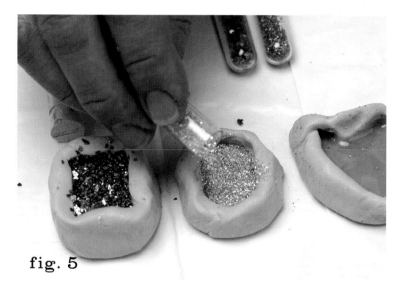

fig. 5

5 Sprinkle coarse- or fine-grit glass glitter onto the new layer of wet resin, being sure to overfill (you want to pack a lot into each mold) **(Fig. 5)**. Dry for 6 hours.

6 Pop your resin druzys out of their molds and you have glittering, natural-looking stones to place into a bezel. Pronged staple bezels (see the images above) work especially well.

6

COOL & COLORFUL:
cold enameling and surface treatments

You're probably familiar with hot enameling, which is a process of melting transparent or opaque glass color onto metal with a torch or in a kiln. By contrast, cold enameling is done by first applying color to your metal, then sealing it with a strong, glasslike stance. No flame is involved in setting the color (only a heat gun for the powder form), and resin is the sealant I use on top of the color. It's simple and low-tech. Using the cold-enameling technique, you can work in layers, adding text, images, texture, photo transfers, and lots of color onto your metalwork to create beautiful finished pieces with depth.

Clear resin is the ideal coating for cold enamel.

Layer cold enameling with paper and clear resin for design impact.

Seal It!

When you're cold enameling, you can use a wide variety of color sources—enamel paint, paper, permanent ink, caulk transfers, photo transfers, rub-ons, oil pastels, colored pencils, crackle enamel, traditional patinas, and more. In one of my workshops, I teach a six-hour accelerated class on metal surface work and patinas. This workshop covers a variety of techniques for achieving great colors, patterns, and surface work on metal in both matte and shiny finishes. My students hear me say over and over again that the secret to a good, long-lasting patina is to apply a solid coat of sealant to protect it. The beauty of using resin as a sealant is that it has glass-like clarity, is simple to apply, and will not wear off over time.

Paper It!

One of my favorite surface treatments is to marry paper with paint onto metal surfaces. My love of doing this in my work stems from having admired the packaging for vintage painted-metal toys, food tins, and hardware. I studied how the layered paint and paper labels survived the wear and tear of a century or more, yet remained clear and intact on metal surfaces. Surely the technique manufacturers used to adhere paint and paper permanently to the surface of metal packaging could be replicated by a jewelry maker! The secret to successfully achieving this effect was simple: resin sealant.

Weather It!

Another vintage look I like to create with enameling on metal is a crackled surface. The look that inspired me was that of a painted barn door, vintage hardware, or lawn furniture that has been weathered by the passage of many seasons. Colors on these aging surfaces crack and flake over time, leaving behind an intriguing

I love creating the effect of weathering with cold enamel on metal.

Create see-through "windows" using resin and colored enamel.

texture. In my hot-enamel work, I always loved re-creating this look, so I was happy to find a simple way to achieve this same effect with cold enameling. Crackling is done by applying two different paints, one at a time. The first paint layer is not compatible with the second, resulting in a surface with an irregular, beautiful crackle. You can find the crackle-surface or second-coat nail polish labeled boldly in the cosmetics section of your local drugstore. These crackle paints are incompatible with any noncrackle nail paint. You must choose your base-coat color wisely to ensure that it will show through well. When the paints are dry, just seal with resin and the crackled color becomes permanent. To create a matte surface, rather than shiny surface, with this technique, sand the dry resin coating lightly until it has the filmy, mysterious look of a worn vintage object.

Make It Negative!

Plique-à-jour, which is French for a "membrane through which passes the light of day," is another enameling technique that can be adapted to cold enameling. In the classic application of this technique, enamel was applied to the openings in metal filigree and fired in a kiln. When finished, light passed through these colorful transparent openings to mimic the look of stained-glass windows. This effect evokes art periods from Old World medieval times to the twentieth-century art nouveau period. Again, the adaptation of this technique to cold enameling is a simple one. Use a premade metal component with cutouts, lay it right side up on top of a piece of clear packing tape, then use a toothpick or clean stir stick to drip colored enamel into the negative spaces. After it dries, remove the packing tape and you'll have those same see-through windows in your piece.

Compartmentalize It!

Cold enameling can also be used to create cloisonné, an ancient enameling technique for decorating and coloring the interior spaces of metal objects or bezels. Traditionally, wire is coiled or segmented into discrete compartments or channels to form a framework for enameling. Then, the wire is firmly fitted into the interior of the metal object or bezel and adhered to it. Next, enamel pastes (a single color or multiple colors) are laid into these compartments, which separate the various color inlays. After firing, the edges of the wire remain a visible decorative element in the finished piece. To make cloisonné with resin, you simply stitute cold enameling for the traditional hot enameling.

I know you'll enjoy the simplicity of cold enameling—no firing needed, just apply and dry. Once you've tried each of these cold-enamel variations, you'll have a great foundation for creating colorful and lasting surface effects on the metal in your jewelry designs.

Resin colored with enamel can be used to create easy-to-make cloissoné.

TECHNIQUE:

Crackle and *Plique-à-Jour* Enameling

MATERIALS & TOOLS

Metal component with cut-outs (e.g., a bezel or frame)

Two-part resin, mixing cups, and stir sticks

Toothpicks

Quick-drying enamel

Crackle enamel nail polish**

Sponge-strip applicator

Fine-grit sandpaper

Cloth wipe

Clear packing tape

Large white plastic trash bag

Alcohol wipes

Baby wipes

Nitrile gloves

**What I love about using nail polish is that (1) the brushes are built in, and (2) it dries quickly.

You'll get color, texture, and transparency when you combine these two enameling techniques in a single piece. Explore this combo to create dynamic, complex surfaces for your jewelry designs. For your metal component, choose from either manufactured pieces or upcycled/found metal objects with cutouts already in them.*

*If you are a more experienced metalworker, you can design and cut out negative spaces from sheet metal using a jeweler's saw.

Before you start, make sure your metal component is clean. (Sand it and wipe it with a cloth, then clean it with alcohol wipes; let it dry.)

Crackling: Place the plastic trash bag on your work surface. Brush a layer of quick-drying enamel onto the front of the component, except for the cutout **(Fig. 1)**. After the first coat dries in about 10 minutes, apply a coat of crackle enamel nail paint as quickly and efficiently as possible on top of the first coat. Dry another 10 minutes. Once this second layer has dried, your component will have a beautiful crackle **(Fig. 2)**. To affix the paint permanently on the metal, apply a very thin coat of resin and dry. Sand lightly if you prefer a matte finish.

Plique-à-jour: Place a piece of clear packing tape onto the back of the cutout(s) in your component, being careful to keep the tape very smooth (you want to avoid pouring the resin into any wrinkles or folds). To put a word and/or a small flat object inside the cutout window, set it onto the tape and press to fix it in place. Mix the resin. Use a sponge applicator to brush the resin on top of the entire piece to coat, including the cutout(s) **(Fig. 3)**. As the negative space fills, you may need to add a bit more resin. Since the back is taped, it will hold the small pool of resin intact until it dries.

Make sure not to overfill the cutouts: The surface should be level and evenly coated. Dry for 6 hours.

If desired, sand the surface lightly to create a matte finish.

*If you are a more experienced metalworker, you can design and cut out negative spaces from sheet metal using a jeweler's saw.

fig. 1

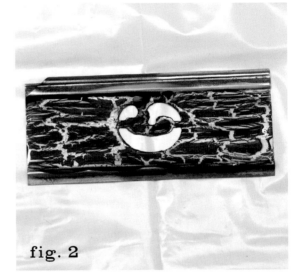

fig. 2

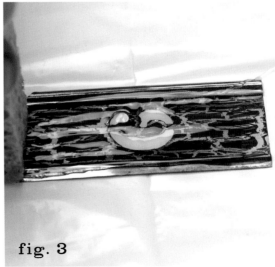

fig. 3

RESIN alchemy

Cold-Enamel
Powder

MATERIALS & TOOLS

Round metal blank

Cold-enamel glue

Cold-enamel powder

Two-part resin, mixing cups, and stir sticks

Sponge-strip applicator

Dapping block with dapping punch

Hammer

Heat gun

Permanent-ink stamp pad

Fine-grit sandpaper

Large white plastic trash bag

Baby wipes

Nitrile gloves

Cold-enamel powder has opened many doors for me in my work. By adding glitter, mica powders, crystal, and/or color to cold-enamel powder, I've been able to re-create the appearance of stones or relics. You can use this form of enamel on any metals other than copper, such as silver, bronze, steel, and so on.

1 Dap the metal blank slightly to cup (refer to the dapping technique on page 56). Sand your metal piece to clean it. Roll cold-enamel glue over all areas on the piece where you would like enamel to adhere (**Fig. 1**).

2 Sprinkle the cold-enamel powder color onto the glue-coated metal surface (**Fig. 2**).

3 Heat the metal surface with the heat gun until the cold-enamel powder melts, about one minute (**Fig. 3**). (These powders have mica flakes and all kinds of interesting inclusions, which add textural dimension.)

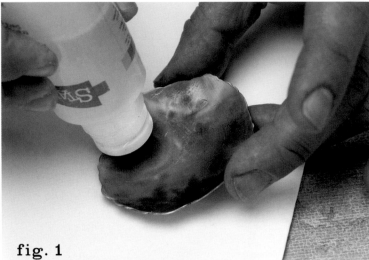

fig. 1

fig. 2

fig. 3

fig. 4

fig. 5

fig. 6

4 To add definition and contrast to the outer edge of your metal component, rub it with a permanent-ink stamp pad **(Fig. 4)**.

5 Mix the resin and apply a very thin layer onto the enameled surface with the sponge applicator **(Fig. 5)**. This gives the enamel surface a nice shine and seals colors permanently. Dry for 6 hours. If you prefer a matte finish, sand your dried piece lightly **(Fig. 6)**.

TIP

Instead of covering the whole surface of a metal blank with enamel powder, you can focus your enameling on a letter, word, numeral, or simple lines. Use a fine-point glue pen to write or sketch onto your piece. (You can also use a small stencil to do this.) Then sprinkle cold-enamel powder over the glue and heat-dry, repeating Steps 3 and 4.

Cloisonné + Mica
Powder

This is a really fun, single-color, cold-enameling technique that can be as detailed or simple as you like. I use fine mica powders, spices, and glitter to re-create an authentic enameled look.

MATERIALS & TOOLS

Large premade round metal bezel

6" (15 cm) of 16- to 18-gauge half-hard wire

Two-part resin, mixing cups, and stir sticks

Toothpick

Mica powders

Reddish spices (cayenne or paprika)

Flat-nose pliers

Hammer

Bench block or anvil

Handheld torch with fuel

Annealing pan and pumice

Fireproof work surface

Heat-resistant tweezers

Quenching pan

Fine-grit sandpaper

Large white plastic trash bag

Baby wipes

Nitrile gloves

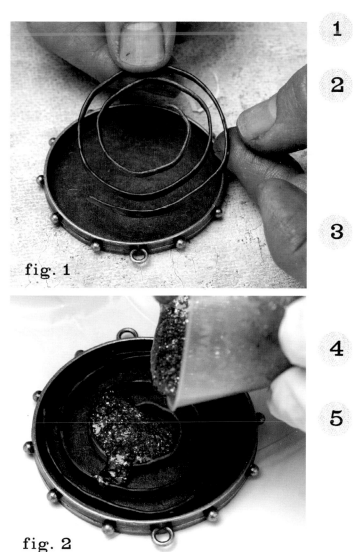

fig. 1

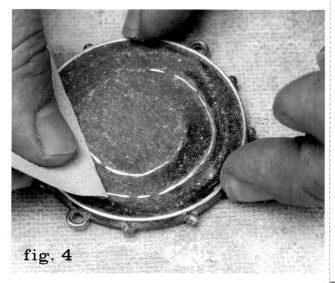

fig. 2

1. Flatten the wire with a hammer. Anneal (see page 54).

2. Form a spiral with the wire using flat-nose pliers, checking to make sure it fits the interior of the bezel. Holding your wire at the midpoint with pliers, lay it inside your bezel (you can use your hands, too) **(Fig. 1)**. The wire forms channels that can be filled with a variety of textures and colors.

3. Place the plastic trash bag on your work surface. Mix the resin, then add spices and dense mica powders; stir until well combined. Slowly pour this mixture into your piece **(Fig. 2)**.

4. When you have finished pouring, remove all visible bubbles by poking them with a tooth-pick **(Fig. 3)**. Dry for 6 hours.

5. When it's dry, sand the surface to expose the top edges of all the internal wire channels and to create a matte finish **(Fig. 4)**. If you prefer a shiny surface, apply another thin layer of resin after sanding and dry for 6 hours.

fig. 3

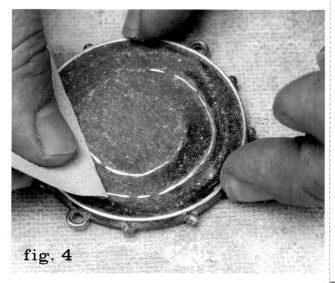

fig. 4

cloisonné + mica powder

Cold-Enamel Head Pins

MATERIALS & TOOLS

One 16" (40.5 cm) piece of 20- to 24-gauge half-hard wire

Two-part resin, mixing cups, and stir sticks

Oil paint, preferably a bright color

Handheld torch and fuel

Annealing pan and pumice

Fireproof work surface

Heat-resistant tweezers

Quenching pan

Round-nose pliers (optional)

Tape

String or wire

Large white plastic trash bags

Baby wipes

Nitrile gloves

I used to create these head pins exclusively in hot enamel, so I loved being able to switch to the ease of a cold-enamel technique instead. Besides doing the practical job of fastening and connecting, enameled head pins become decorative elements that add juicy bits of color to any design. Using oil paint to color your resin creates bright translucency.

Cut your wire into four 4"
(10 cm) pieces. Using your torch,
draw a bead on one end of a
piece of wire to create a small
ball. Quench (see page 54).
Repeat with the remaining three
wire pieces. To make the balls
without a torch, roll one end of
each piece of wire into a tight
ball using round-nose pliers. Set
aside.

fig. 1

2 Place the plastic trash bag on
your work surface. Mix the
resin, then add a tiny bit of oil
paint; stir to combine thoroughly (add a little bit more paint if
you want to deepen the color)
(Fig. 1).

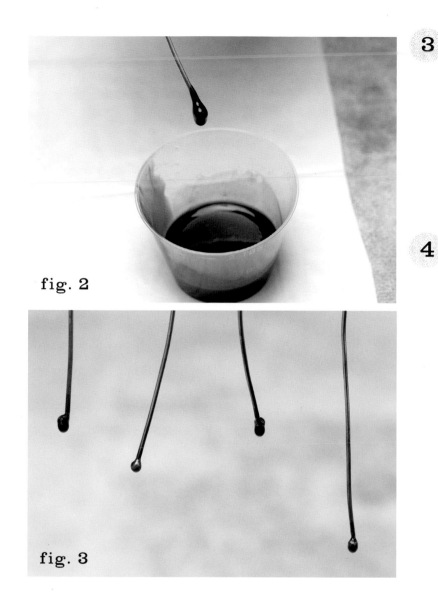

fig. 2

fig. 3

3   Dip the ball end of one head pin into the colored resin mixture **(Fig. 2)**. After you dip it, hang up the freshly coated head pin to dry by taping it to a stretched, suspended piece of string or wire. Place a trash bag beneath the head pin to catch the resin drips. Repeat with remaining three head pins.

4   Repeat this process three or four times with each head pin until a large ball of colored resin forms on each **(Fig. 3)**. (*Note:* Working in a room that is 70°F (21°C) or cooler will help the resin thicken and accumulate into a ball.)

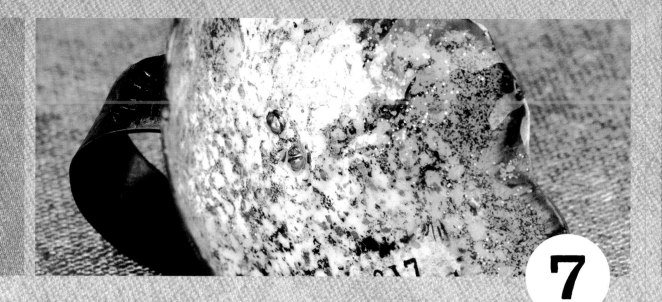

NO MISTAKES:
finishes + fixes

You may be surprised to learn that resin and many other mixed-media materials can be treated much like metalwork. Just as with metal, you must file, sand, polish, drill, saw, and clean your resin to give it a satisfyingly professional finish.

Start to Finish

When I pull a dry resin piece out of a rubber mold, this is just the beginning. I now add finishing touches that will make my creation come to life! I fill in seams, file off excess resin, rub color into cracks and crevices to make them stand out, and polish or apply a final coat of resin for shine and as a protective sealant. To review, the following are a few basic finishing techniques and tips to make the most of your resin art.

TRIMMING AND FILING. When resin overflows a bezel or frame, you can wipe up the spill with a damp paper towel. However, if the resin has dried already, it's also easy to fix. You can snip off the excess with scissors or metal shears (for thicker amounts). Next, file to clean resin off any metal pieces you didn't intend to coat. Always file away from you. To do this, rest your piece flat against a bench pin or table. With the piece extending slightly over the edge, file in long downward strokes. Use a larger file if there is a lot of resin to be filed away and a small needle file for tiny projects and projects with a lot of detail. Choose a file shape—round, square, or flat—compatible with the grooves, edges, and surfaces you need to file clean.

SANDING AND POLISHING. Once you have finished filing your piece, if you want to smooth its surface more, sand it with a 500-grit paper. To restore the shine after sanding, buff out your piece on a jeweler's wheel for a polished smooth look. If you don't have a jeweler's wheel, you can use a buffing attachment on a Dremel tool.

PATINAS. After filing and sanding, it's time to rub a patina into depressed or raised areas so you can highlight them (just as with metalwork). I like to use my fingers to rub brown acrylic paint into them. Then, I rub off the excess with a wet paper towel. (The paint washes off my hands

File to clean any overflow dried resin.

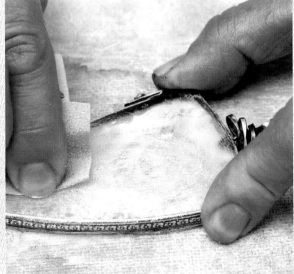

Smooth your resin surface by sanding, then buff to a shine.

To add patina, I use my finger to rub acrylic paint into scored lines.

easily.) Often I rub in a secondary color with gilder's paste, a waxlike substance that is harder to spread. Besides having a beautiful metallic undertone, gilder's paste gives a durable finish—which is especially good if you don't plan to seal your piece.

RESIN COATING. To preserve a beautiful patina, coat the surface of your piece one final time with a very thin layer of resin. I like to apply it with a throwaway paintbrush or sponge strip. This is an optional step, but it does help to keep your patina just right and can turn a matte surface back into a super-shiny resin piece.

FIXES. When you work with resin for the first time, take some time to perfect mixing two-part resin. Also, try it out on inexpensive bezels. Practicing like this will help you sidestep a lot of common errors. After you have poured resin into a bezel and the resin is thoroughly dry, check for overpours, bubbles, and other common

problems. You can drill into embedded bubbles and refill them with fresh resin. Simply use a toothpick to place a drop of resin in each hole (add another drop, if necessary). Use that same toothpick to work the resin all the way into the hole. When it dries, your surface will be smooth and you won't see any bubbles.

Once in a great while, one of my students pours resin into a beautiful, expensive silver bezel and makes a big mistake. The only way to remove dried resin is with a very toxic product called ATTACK, available at hardware stores. It dissolves resin and leaves your metal intact. Only resort to this if you are desperate to salvage a special metal piece.

SAFE CLEANUP. When doing any type of cleanup work, make sure that the area you are working in is well-ventilated and wear a respirator mask. Airborne particles from any material are toxic and carcinogens. I have a vacuum conveniently attached to my resin workbench for regular cleanups.

If you spill wet resin on a floor, you can wipe it up. However, consider spreading a plastic painting tarp on the area under and around your worktable when you're working with resin and paints so you won't have to worry about spillage.

After all the resin techniques you've learned from *Resin Alchemy*, it's worth repeating that you can fix almost any mistake you make with resin. So be intrepid! Make some exciting trial-and-error discoveries with this magical medium. And enjoy the many discoveries you'll make.

RESOURCES

You'll find the following websites are some of the most comprehensive for sourcing tools and materials to make amazing resin art.

Websites

ICERESIN.COM

This is my find-everything store where you can buy jeweler's-grade crystal-clear, nontoxic resin, and learn from my free instructional videos and blogs. Lots of components, especially bezels, and new products such as Iced Enamels for cold-enamel resin work.

FIREMOUNTAINGEMS.COM

Fire Mountain Gems and Beads is a favorite site for resin, jewelry components, gemstones, tools, and more.

RIOGRANDE.COM

Rio Grande Jewelry Supplies offers one-stop shopping for jewelry makers: metals, tools, jewelry components, plus free instructional videos.

IJSINC.COM

Indian Jewelers Supply Company is a longtime New Mexico source for metal, tools, components, bezels, and gemstones.

METALLIFEROUS.COM

The Metalliferous brick-and-mortar store is a New York City destination for metalworkers. On their website, find extensive jewelry supplies that include interesting components and bezels.

ARTMECHANIQUE.COM

Art Mechanique offers stylish and unique jewelry components and bezels.

COOLTOOLS.US

Since I love working with bronze and base metal and decorative bezel wire, Cool Tools is a great site to load up on those supplies.

FAUXBONE.COM

Find a variety of tools and supplies on the Faux Bone site for cutting, filing, and working with resin plastic and metal. Artist Robert Dancik's Faux Bone product is the standout: it's a nontoxic, high-grade rigid PVC that, when heated, can be shaped every which way.

JEWELRYTOOLS.COM

Their tagline is "Every tool you need and then some." Locate what you're looking for among 5,000+ in-stock tools.

Susan Lenart Kazmer Books & DVDs

Making Connections: A Handbook of Cold Joins for Jewelers and Mixed-Media Artists—Book by Susan Lenart Kazmer (Interweave)

Metalwork: Making Cold Connections with Rivets—DVD by Susan Lenart Kazmer (Interweave)

Exploring Resin Jewelry Making—DVD by Susan Lenart Kazmer (Interweave)

INDEX

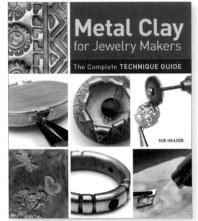